THE KEY
TO THE
CASTLE

The Key to the Castle

Zen and Travel Stories of Trust

JOURNEYS PRESS

Sue Schleifer

Copyright © 2013 by Sue Schleifer

All rights reserved

No part of this book may be reproduced or transmitted in any form or by any means, electronic or mechanical, including photocopying, recording, or by any information storage and retrieval system, without permission in writing from the publisher. For permission requests, write to the address below:

Journeys Press
2851 Johnston Street, Suite 207
Lafayette, LA 70503

www.facebook.com/KeyToTheCastleBook

Cover and book design by Megan Barra

Photograph of the author by Robin May
All other photos by Sue Schleifer

ISBN 978-0-9890762-0-3

Excerpts from *The Dharma Mirror,* and "The Human Route," by Zen Master Seung Sahn, copyright © Kwan Um School of Zen, are reprinted by permission of the Kwan Um School of Zen.

I'll Fly Away, Albert E. Brumley
© Copyright 1932 in "Wonderful Message" by Hartford Music Co. Renewed 1960 by Albert E. Brumley & Sons/SESAC (admin by ClearBox Rights). All rights reserved. Used by permission.

Printed in the United States of America

For Mark, my husband and fellow traveler, with whom I have learned to love and be loved. Our journey continues. Thank you for inviting me to join you in practice at the Empty Gate Zen Center.

Introduction

My lanky sister Betty, the oldest and tallest of our band of three musketeers, walked at the front of our line carrying a spindly stick she picked up on the bank of the creek that ran beside our house. The youngest, I followed next. Bringing up the rear was our family friend, Masha. Most Saturdays we took the dirt path that led from our back yard to Stevens Park and into the Santa Barbara hills. Sometimes, instead of taking the path, we cautiously stepped from rock to rock up the dry creek bed shaded by oak and sycamore trees. We were explorers.

We climbed to the top of huge boulders where we discovered smooth holes carved from years of Chumash Indians grinding acorns on the slabs. Sometimes we were surprised by a snake on the trail that shook its angry rattler at us. We ran all the way back home in fear and collapsed on the shaded lawn where it was safe to breathe and explode with laughter.

As a teenager, and after my sister went off exploring with her own friends, my girlfriends and I rode our bikes the four miles one-way to Hendry's beach. We took long walks, talking and sifting through the ups and downs of our lives. We were forever cooking up elaborate plans. One such plan was to roller skate to our first day of high school. We were not accomplished roller skaters and this was before the days of roller blades, so it proved to be a long and bumpy trip. We laughed, took some spills and were surprised how far it was to our new school. We arrived late to the first day of high school.

Adventures continued until the final day of summer prior to senior year of high school. On that Sunday, we rode our bikes to Montecito and ended up at Butterfly Beach. We sat on the rock wall watching the crashing waves until the sun set and the moon rose on the ocean's horizon.

We composed a ditty with a bouncing rhythm, "Does the moonlight tan you in the summertime? Does the moonlight tan you in the fall, fall, fall? (In turn we leaned to the right from the waist and across each other's lap as one at a time we shouted "fall.") Does the moonlight tan you in the summertime? Does the moonlight tan you at all?"

We were postponing our final year of high school for as long as we possibly could. Though we didn't talk about it, I think we were afraid that our adventures would soon be ending.

What we didn't know or believe on that summer day was that the adventures would not end. Instead, my childhood in Santa Barbara set the stage for the journeys that followed. My travels have taken me to Nepal and to France; Thailand and England; Bali and Canada. Whether hiking, biking, riding on the back of an elephant or in a rickety bus, the journeys led me to places I could never have imagined. On each trip I reflected on my life and the lives of the people I met. "What is it like to live here?" "Who am I?" "What is going on here?"

Later I learned that these are also questions that I would reflect on while sitting in meditation at a Zen retreat. "What am I?" "What is this?" And discover the answer, "Don't know."

This book captures many of my outward and inward journeys. As a beginning student of Zen, I hope my experiences on the meditation cushion will serve as an introduction to others who may be curious about Zen and meditation. And along the way, I'll share some of my travel stories that line the path of this life-long journey.

First Meditation Retreat

In 1995 in Berkeley, California my boyfriend, Mark, asked me to join him at a one-day Zen retreat held in a rented church sanctuary. Mark and I had been seeing one another for a few months. We met in a four-week zydeco dance class taught by Dana DeSimone at what was then Studio Z.

The class was fun and prepared me for the Cajun and zydeco dances that I started to attend at local venues in the San Francisco Bay Area, including Ashkenaz Music and Dance Community Center, where many years later I would become the Executive Director.

Mark says he took note of me in that zydeco dance class but I didn't take much notice of him. It wasn't until several months later that we met again at a zydeco dance at the Berkeley Square on a Saturday afternoon. This venue normally featured rock or punk bands, but for some reason on that December afternoon, they hosted a zydeco dance. Mark asked me to dance and after a two-step and a waltz, we began to talk. He had just returned from the Society for Ethnomusicology conference in Milwaukee. I told him that my friend Lily had also been at that conference. Lily became the magnet for Mark and me in our conversation that day.

Our next "date" was a New Year's Eve zydeco dance in Alameda. Most memorable from that night was that Mark picked me up in a station wagon that had a child's seat in the back. He hadn't told me he had kids. As we approached the venue I finally got up the courage to ask if he was a father. He looked at me surprised and then informed me he was house-sitting for his professor and had been given license to use the car too.

Over the next few months, in addition to dancing, we went hiking, shared meals and slowly began to get to know one another. Mark, being a man of few spoken words, did not tell me much about what would take place at the Zen retreat, and I didn't ask many questions, at least about that.

The main thing I recall about that first retreat was that at certain points during the 30-minute sitting periods, the Zen Master stood up and ceremoniously picked up a long wooden stick and walked slowly in front of the seated meditators. If the person sitting gave a slight bow when the Zen Master walked past, he hit the person on each shoulder blade with the stick. I didn't understand this at all. Why would anyone want to be hit with a stick? What exactly is going on here? Is this a cult?

I never bowed to be hit with the stick during that retreat. After all, I wasn't a masochist. While I didn't have much difficulty sitting on the cushion that day, I also don't recall that the retreat was very significant. It just seemed like something new to try because my boyfriend asked me to join him.

Backroads

I started bicycling in the hills and pedaling longer distances after "Carl," my housemate at the time, invited me to ride on the back of his tandem bicycle. We headed up into the hills above Oakland. I couldn't believe how easily we climbed the steep, curvy roads. He was definitely putting more power into the pedaling than I was. Through riding with Carl, I gained strength and learned cycling technique. When I got back on my own bike, I knew more about when to shift, how to stand up in the pedals and make turns on curvy roads.

It was from Carl's friends that I first learned about Backroads Bicycle Touring (as it was called in the early days of the company). I poured over the Backroads catalog and decided to go on the only trip that fit into my schedule and price range: Bryce, Zion, and Grand Canyon camping trip in late September 1986. This happened to be one of the most challenging cycling trips in the catalog. Fortunately, I knew I could climb into the van if I wanted to.

I took a welcome week off from the job I hated as a Training Specialist for a large company. I flew from Oakland to Las Vegas and was picked up by the Backroads van that took us to a campground at Cedar Breaks National Monument in Utah. That night was so cold that we held the baked potatoes in our hands to warm up. In the morning I reached for my water bottle only to find that the water had frozen.

Our small group of eight guests and three leaders shivered as we jumped on our bikes and quickly descended more than 4000 feet. It would never be that cold again on that trip. We cycled long distances from park to park, including Bryce Canyon with its red spires and on to the majestic north rim of the Grand Canyon. As I cycled for many lonely and challenging miles I had lots of time to think. It became clear to me that I needed to quit my job even if I wasn't sure of my new direction.

While I was trying to figure out what to do next, I registered with a few temp agencies and went out on jobs. I thought, "If I am working in these funky temp jobs, I might as well work for a company that I care about." So, I called the office manager at Backroads. I explained that I had been on a Backroads trip recently, and that I was in between jobs. I wondered if they could use some temporary help. Mary asked me to come in to interview the next day.

The office was located in a semi-abandoned shopping strip in San Leandro, California. I met with Mary and owner, Tom Hale, and I was soon offered a job. It was my third day on the job when Suzy, one of the trip leaders, asked me if I wanted to lead trips. I said, "No." I didn't see myself being on the road away from home for days on end, nor did I see myself as a bike "jock" or as a "leader."

A week later, they were in a pinch and needed someone to co-lead a weekend trip in the Santa Ynez Valley. This was not the customary way that leaders were hired then or now. I found myself "leading" this trip with Jim. All I can say is that I couldn't have been luckier than to have Jim as my co-leader as he really did most of the work and was incredibly good natured about it. I wasn't strong or tall enough to lift the bikes over my head and slip them into the racks on top of the tall van while standing on my tippy toes on top of a step stool. I also didn't know how to do much in the way of bike maintenance. As we readied the bikes for the guests each morning and I looked at my greasy hands, Jim gave me advice, or perhaps a warning, that stood me well over the years, "you're gonna get dirty."

At that time, I had no idea that I would travel all over the world with Backroads. I occasionally led trips, but mostly I researched new destinations and evaluated existing trips. Working in the office I learned about negotiations, planning and analysis, leadership, entrepreneurship, and made life-long friends. Backroads became my life, my work and my community for many years.

One never knows the twists and turns that our lives will take if we are open to following the paths that present themselves.

Going on Retreat

I have gone on many different types of retreats over the years. These included work retreats where we left our normal surroundings to gather for an afternoon or a couple of days to look creatively at the organization and to come up with new plans or strategies. One of my favorite work retreats was held after I had been employed at Backroads for a few years. The leadership team met in a private room at a gourmet restaurant in Marin County. During the two day strategic planning retreat we also enjoyed delicious meals.

Backroads was and is a company that designs and takes guests on luxury bicycling and hiking vacations to beautiful locations around the world. They definitely know how to pamper their guests and employees and also challenge them to "perform" at their best.

Besides work retreats I have treated myself to personal retreats when I wanted time for contemplation. I took several of these retreats at San Francisco Zen Center locations: Tassajara in the Carmel Valley and Green Gulch Farm Zen Center in Marin County, both in California. I chose them because of their beauty and serenity and because I liked being around people who were practicing meditation, even if I didn't spend much time meditating with them.

I went on at least one of these retreats when I was working for Backroads. In 1995 I was experiencing very painful shingles centered in my lower back. While the pain was beginning to diminish, I decided to go on a personal retreat to contemplate how to get my health back on track. Mark and our friends Linda and Patrick and I attended the Sunday morning Dharma Talk at Green Gulch and then they left me there alone for two nights.

I meandered through the extensive organic gardens, walked the trail to Muir Beach, relaxed on the sand and watched the waves, wrote in my journal, sat in meditation, ate vegetarian meals in the dining room with the residents in silence, and paid attention to my thoughts and feelings. On the bulletin board outside the Green Gulch office I noticed a flyer for a pottery class. The class was to start in a couple of weeks on Saturday mornings at Green Gulch.

I took a copy of the flyer home with me. The sheet described that we would dig our own clay out of the hills at Green Gulch farm. We would then work with the clay to make it useable for making tea bowls. I decided to take the six-week class. It meant getting up early on Saturday mornings, driving an hour from Berkeley across the Richmond/San Rafael Bridge and on the winding road to Green Gulch. It was September, but often cold, drizzly and foggy in the mornings. Upon arrival, I walked briskly from the parking area down the eucalyptus tree-lined dirt road in dense fog, bundled up in a fleece jacket, hat, gloves, and boots to the cottage that would become a refuge for a few hours.

During the first class, we hiked to a hillside from which we dug the red clay. In the weeks that the clay was being shaped from earth to suitable pottery material, we were given clay that had already been transformed. We learned how to shape the simple and elegant hand pottery tea bowl forms that our teacher shared with us.

Each week, our teacher began the class at a leisurely pace. She even seemed to talk slowly. At Backroads, we worked at an often feverish pace. Since I had begun working there, I had learned to talk, walk, and work quickly as we had much to do (or so we thought). So on Saturday mornings, I was still in my fast mode. I got annoyed by how slowly the class got started and progressed. I was frustrated.

But then something happened. I slowed down. I allowed myself to just be in that cold room at Green Gulch and put my hands around the clay and relax. By the fourth class I was in a groove. The drive helped me to slow down from my fast-paced week and it continued as I worked with the clay and listened to the minimal instructions of the teacher and the quiet conversations of my classmates.

During the fifth class, I had something special to share with my classmates. The night before, during an exquisitely planned and prepared dinner, Mark asked me to marry him.

I accepted.

With their hands covered in red clay, my classmates clapped.

This was a journey from the pain of shingles, to a personal retreat at Green Gulch where I noticed a flyer, to a tea bowl pottery class where I practiced slowing down, to marriage.

Marriage

The person we chose to officiate at our wedding was Jeff Kitzes, Zen Master Bon Soeng. I didn't know him well at that point, but I had a good feeling about him from the twinkle in his blue eyes to his rosy cheeks. He was the person who led the very first Zen retreat I attended. After that first retreat day, I occasionally joined Mark on Saturday mornings or Wednesday nights for sitting in meditation at the Empty Gate Zen Center.

Marriage was especially significant for me as I was 44 years old. I had lived a full life, traveled throughout the world, had many interesting jobs, and during those years often yearned for a lifelong partner. Mark too had never been married. He was seven years younger than me, a graduate student finishing his PhD. I now had a good job. While we were at different points in our lives, we took the leap of faith and trusted that we would make the marriage work.

Mark and I planned and wrote the wedding ceremony including our vows. Each year on our anniversary, our ritual is to read the vows aloud to each other in unison. We have read our vows on beaches in Santa Barbara and Maui, at Lake Tahoe, sitting on a bench dodging light rain showers in Lithia Park in Ashland, Oregon, and in the backyard of various homes.

Wedding Vows

Mark I declare my love for you today and every day.

I promise to share with you
- my joys and sorrows,
- dreams and fears,
- achievements and disappointments,
- laughter and tears,
- and passion for love and life.

I commit myself to support you through hard times, and to join you in being there for our friends, family, and the community in which we live.

I will keep
- an open mind that tries new things,
- an inquiring mind that learns from you,
- a humble mind that knows when to compromise,
- and an independent mind that knows when to go its own way.

Though we may not walk the same spiritual path, I will be a loving witness to your journey.

I vow
- to spend the rest of my life with you
- to have fun and
- to celebrate life with you at every opportunity.

At the time we wrote our vows, Mark was a practicing Lutheran and also practiced Zen. I was a "cultural" Jew. Though we didn't know this would happen at the time, we have watched as our spiritual paths have merged.

Our parents were able to come to our wedding and Mark's father and my mother read passages at the ceremony. Mark's father did not live to see him receive his doctorate. A few years later, my mom would not have been able to read her passage in front of a crowd.

Zydeco dancing at our wedding

What is Going on Here?

Not long after we married, Mark was offered a one-year university teaching assignment in Ohio. After nine years, I was ready to quit my job at Backroads, so we made the move. The teaching assignment ended up being two years. Then, as is often the case for "young" academics, Mark was out of a job. I wasn't wedded to my job in Ohio so we decided to move back to the Bay Area in California. We drove across country stopping in Santa Barbara to visit my mom before heading north. Something didn't seem quite right at my mom's house.

The house was dirty and in a bit of disarray. Mom was clear in her conversations at some times and at other times would ask us the same questions repeatedly. What is going on? I noticed stacks of paper on the floor in her bedroom. So when she was taking a walk around the neighborhood one afternoon I decided to look around more closely. I found bills that appeared to be unpaid. When I asked her about the bills she told me that a nice lady at the bank would help her sometimes. We went to see the lady at the bank and I began to get a clearer picture of what was going on.

WHAT IS GOING ON HERE?

This was the start of a journey that I had not anticipated nor planned. It was not a journey that I would choose again though it is one from which I have learned more than I could have imagined at the time.

Mark and I never did make it back to the Bay Area to live, at least not for another two years. Once we realized that mom was in the beginning stages of dementia, we decided to stay with her and do our best to take care of her.

Sometimes my best wasn't so good. I got frustrated with her inability to say what she was thinking. "Mom, use your words." My patience felt endlessly tried when she would ask the same question over and over at the dinner table. I found carrots in the freezer and 200 pounds of rocks in the trunk of her car. She picked incessantly at her face and washed her hands repeatedly. I could not for the longest time get into my head and heart that this was dementia and not mom purposely trying to drive me crazy.

When the neurologist, after a verbal cognitive test, told mom and me that she was most likely in the early to mid-stages of Alzheimer's disease, mom had no reaction. I suppose by then she didn't remember what Alzheimer's disease was. I knew what it was and the tears came to my eyes though I already suspected the diagnosis prior to his telling us.

So we muddled through. We had good days and not so good days. At the grocery store and around town, I noticed other adults with their aging parents. We took mom out to hear live music, something that we all enjoyed. We went for walks on the beach and out to dinner once a week. She was eating healthier now that Mark and I were doing most of the cooking.

One time I took her to see a dance performance by the group,

Urban Bush Women. On the drive home, mom asked me for the fifth time, "What was the name of that group?" When I told her, she said, "Those words don't go together." I was amazed. The English teacher in her was still active. How could her mind work so well tonight and be all confused earlier in the day? It was a mystery.

This journey didn't end when Mark and I decided that we were not able to continue the daily care of mom after two years. We moved her out of her home and into my younger brother's house for seven months. Then he and my sister-in-law moved her to a board and care facility on the central coast of California.

Now living back in the San Francisco Bay Area, I drove the five hours to visit her and each time observed as her mind declined until she no longer spoke much. When I came into the room and said cheerfully, "Hi Mom," her face lit up. I always suspected that she would do that with anyone who walked into the room and said "Hi Mom."

My heart ached on these visits and during the time in between. I was in a perpetual state of sadness. Were we doing the right things for her? How best to care for her and care for ourselves? These were tough questions with no correct answers.

Empty Gate Zen Center

The Empty Gate Zen Center is an urban Zen Center in the heart of Berkeley, California on a street with houses, apartment buildings, a church, and a halfway house that keeps noisy geese.

The center consists of an entryway, a small kitchen, a lounge area with two small half bathrooms on either side and a separate shower area. Down the hall is a room where the Zen Master gives interviews and where he also conducts his private psychotherapy practice when not on retreat. A small room that serves as the Zen Center office also has a sleeping bunk in a loft. On many of the walls throughout the center hang grey robes from pegs. A small name tag above the peg indicates whose robe is hanging in that spot.

At the end of the hall is the dharma room where we practice meditation. The walls are white; the floor is hardwood. The mahogany altar is topped with a gold Buddha sitting on a red cushion. Zen-style paintings hang on the walls as well as photos of the founding teachers. A large clapperless bell hangs from a stand in the corner. Deep rust-colored square mats with dark blue cushions atop them are set in a square pattern around the room. A screen hides shelving where additional cushions and chairs are kept.

When sitting in the dharma room, we can hear the noise of cars, sirens, people talking as they walk down the street, a rooster rising, and sometimes homeless people mumbling out loud to themselves.

Empty Gate Zen Center was founded in 1977 by Zen Master Seung Sahn from South Korea. It is one of more than 100 international centers that make up the Kwan Um School of Zen. He started the first temple in 1972 in Providence, Rhode Island and that continues today as the international head temple.

Empty Gate Zen Center dharma room

From the Kwan Um School of Zen website:

> The heart of the Kwan Um School of Zen is the practice. Zen Master Seung Sahn very simply taught "Don't Know". This means, in each moment to open unconditionally to all that presents itself to us. By doing this, our innate wisdom and compassion will naturally breathe and flow into our lives.
>
> The Zen centers of the Kwan Um School of Zen around the world offer training in Zen meditation through instruction, daily morning and evening meditation practice, public talks, teaching interviews, retreats, workshops, and community living. Our programs are open to anyone regardless of previous experience.
>
> The School's purpose is to make this practice of Zen as accessible as possible. It is our wish to help human beings find their true direction and vow to save all beings from suffering.

Zen Master Bon Soeng (Jeff Kitzes) has been the guiding teacher of Empty Gate Zen Center since 1992. Like me, he was raised in a Jewish family. He began practicing Zen in 1975. He is married, has a cat, a full gray beard, enjoys reading about politics and watching golf on television. In his psychotherapy practice he specializes in the integration of Zen Buddhism and western psychotherapy.

Soon after we moved back to the Bay Area, after our sojourn in Santa Barbara taking care of my mom, I started to attend the

Empty Gate Zen Center's Wednesday night sessions on a regular basis. In addition to chanting and sitting for 25 minutes, a student in the school gave a Dharma talk and then Zen Master Bon Soeng expanded on the talk, followed by a question and answer period. I enjoyed these talks and the teachings by the Zen Master. I began to understand a bit more about Zen, about the practice of sitting in meditation, and the idea of observing one's mind. I found comfort at the Zen Center as I was asking questions about my mom and how to best care for her from a distance.

Zen Master Bon Soeng (Jeff Kitzes)

Spontaneity in Bali

I was riding "sweep," bicycling with or behind the last guest to ensure his safety on a Backroads bicycle tour in Bali. The other guests on the trip were ahead of us and my co-leader and our Balinese driver and guide were in the van ready to dispense water, snacks or give someone a lift. The road was narrow and lined with tree ferns, huge palms and brilliant green tropical vegetation that felt cooling despite the extreme heat and humidity. As we steadily climbed, sweat trickled down our faces from under our bicycle helmets and our shirts clung to our bodies. It was a typical Balinese day in May, 80 degrees Fahrenheit with 80% humidity so that when it started to rain, it was a welcome relief.

As I rode beside "David," we saw just ahead of us a skinny Balinese man on a no-speed bicycle. The rain came down so hard we could barely see that he dropped his bike on the side of the road and headed down the slick slope. Without thinking I motioned to David, as he wouldn't have been able to hear me even if I had tried to speak, to come with me as I followed the Balinese man. We set our bikes down on the edge of the road and slipped our way down the muddy hill.

We discovered the Balinese bicyclist standing under an open structure, four bamboo supports with a thatched roof and a cement floor. Under this same dry structure were three Balinese men and one woman also taking advantage of the shelter. They didn't seem too surprised to see us as we joined them in our mutual desire to take refuge from the intense rainstorm. Beads of rain dripped from our bodies and our hair as we smiled at the others.

Next to our structure was a second similar shelter with a man and woman steadily working and barely noticing our presence. They kept a fire going in a heavily blackened stone fireplace. The man held a bamboo stick onto which was tied a piece of metal that he turned and worked in the fire. The woman pumped a bellows. The man quickly turned the stick and shaped the metal into a knife. How hot this ancient work of smelting a knife was even on a rainy afternoon.

When the heavy rain stopped, David and I said goodbye to our shelter companions and crawled up the muddy slope to retrieve our bikes.

As I pedaled down the road, I realized that had we not been riding our bikes at the same pace as the Balinese man, had it not started to rain in sheets, had we not spontaneously followed him, we would not have witnessed this intimate view of daily Balinese life. It is one of my strongest memories from my trip to Bali in 1988.

What is it about travel that makes it easier to be spontaneous, to follow our hunches and take risks? In my daily life, with all the responsibilities and schedules, it is harder for me to go off on an unintended path. While on vacation, my days are more leisurely, my eyes are wide open for the newness of it all, and I am eager to learn and take it in.

SPONTANEITY IN BALI

Zen Master Bon Soeng gave a talk in Singapore and parts of it are excerpted on the Empty Gate Zen Center website. *True Self, Authentic Self* begins,

> This talk is inspired by the life of Zen Master Seung Sahn. Through his teachings and his action he was a consistent example of authenticity. Being with him would shake the foundations of my "I, my, me" mind. Things would feel surreal; my usual evaluation and control would loosen. In its place would appear spontaneity and humor. He showed me how one can be committed to a vow of service to the world while at the same time completely enjoying the moment. His teaching expressed spontaneity, a moment centered life lived with the purpose of attaining true self and helping this world.

From Zen Master Bon Soeng and from sitting in meditation, I too am learning how to be awake for the daily journeys, not just those experienced on a rainy afternoon on the island of Bali.

Ritual in Bali

I have never enjoyed the question, "what is the favorite place you have traveled?" But when pressed, I usually reply, Bali.

What is it about Bali that is so magical? For me it is the beauty of the landscape: green and fertile. Every meter seemingly cultivated and groomed with terraces of rice fields. As we rode our bicycles, we saw men using a sickle to keep the grasses along the roadside under control. Everything seemed to grow so quickly.

I was entranced by the beauty of the people too, their welcoming smiles and shouts of "Hallo!" "Where you from?" "Where you go?" as we rode down the road. School children in uniforms waived to us. Women wore plumeria flowers in their hair and wrapped themselves in colorful batik sarongs. They walked gracefully with small steps balancing tall offerings of fruit and flowers on their heads as they headed to their local temple on a festival day, which seemed to be often.

Each day, they made small, intricately woven pieces of bamboo or leaves, with a bit of rice and flowers artfully arranged atop them. Then these offerings were placed rather unceremoniously on the ground where dogs would eat them or they could be stepped upon. The offerings are meant to protect their home or business from evil spirits.

Several times during my trips to Bali, I felt sacredness in the air and tears would well up in my eyes. I visited the Elephant Cave carved out of a large rock wall. Inside were shrines visited by ascetics in the 11th century. As I stood at the entrance taking in both the details and the whole impact of the carved stone elephant, I was overcome with deep reverence and awe.

I also felt awe when I watched the gamelan orchestras and elaborately dressed dancers. I loved the sound of the clanging of the ornate instruments and was entranced by the precise and agile movements of the young dancers.

I bought several textile pieces – woven ikat and colorful batik sarongs which I still decorate my home with today. I experienced Bali as a sensory delight. During the last few days of the bike trip, as we rode through villages, we saw men constructing gigantic paper maché figures. And on the last day of the trip, we witnessed everyone dressed in their finest clothes, carrying their offerings to the temple. The temples were colorfully decorated with cloth, umbrellas and flowers in preparation for Nyepi Day, the Balinese New Year.

That night, back at our hotel, and after the bicycle trip had ended, I sat with the two trip leaders. We were ready to head to bed, when we heard sounds of clanging outside. It sounded like a procession. So we put on our shoes and headed outside to investigate.

We joined in the procession of boys and men as they headed down to the beach. The boys shot off loud firecrackers and men carried one of the large paper maché statues that we had seen being constructed earlier in the week. The statue was placed on a platform attached to two long bamboo poles on either side. Six men on each side balanced the platform on their shoulders. We followed them down a dirt road as they carefully placed the statue on the beach. A priest said a blessing and they made an offering. Then they set the large statue, and other smaller ones, on fire. The heads burned first, with ashes flying everywhere. Into the dark sky, they dragged the burning statues into the ocean. I imagined the structures as pirate ships burning in the sea.

Abruptly, everyone disappeared. We stood on the beach mesmerized and then realized that most everyone was gone. The next day was Nyepi Day, a Hindu holiday of silence, meditation and fasting. No one was supposed to be out on the streets. The authorities did give special permission for hotels to serve their guests food.

While we didn't spend the next day in complete silence, I did appreciate a day of quiet and inactivity. Today if I were in Bali on Nyepi Day, after having practiced Zen, I probably would spend the day in silence, meditation and fasting.

Nyepi Day Sculpture

First Day-Long Silent Retreat

Sitting a one day retreat from 9 a.m. – 4:30 p.m. when I was 42 years old and sitting from 6 a.m. – 9:30 p.m. when I was 53 years old was a completely different experience. In the shorter day of an informal silent retreat, the schedule includes 108 bows, eight 30-minute sitting periods, six 10-minute walking meditation periods, no chanting, and one informal meal. During a "regular" retreat day that lasts from 6:00 a.m. – 9:30 p.m., we perform 108 bows, sit thirteen 30-minute periods, do nine 10-minute walking meditation sessions, chant a total of 90 minutes, and eat three formal meals with work periods and breaks sprinkled in-between.

The combination of the longer day, more sitting periods, formal meals, all of the chanting and an older body contributed to a much greater challenge for me.

After the first formal meal, I worked myself up into a thinking frenzy: "The way we clean our bowls is ridiculous. This is the 21st century for god's sake. We can wash the damn bowls in the sink with hot water and soap rather than using our fingers and hot tea. This method is unsanitary. We aren't living as monks in Korea. What is the point?"

I talked with Zen Master Bon Soeng about it during my interview. He was very patient with me. He said he didn't recall anyone getting sick from the way we cleaned our bowls.

My body was sore and I thought I might crawl out of my skin by the end of the evening. The chanting seemed to go on forever. "Why in the world are we chanting the *Heart Sutra* and the *Great Dharani* again? We already did that once tonight."

I couldn't wait to leave when 9:30 p.m. finally came around. I made a quick exit from the Zen Center barely saying good-bye to anyone. When I arrived home I told Mark, "I have no idea why I did that." That night I did not see attending another all day retreat in my future.

However, over the next couple of years, I participated in two more retreats – I sat a day and a half of a three day retreat and one full day of an eight-day retreat. Some part of me felt called to take a break from my normal schedule, sit down and be with other people in meditation. The next couple of retreats were a bit easier for me than the first. I didn't fight the retreat forms as much and just tried to be there and watch my mind. I couldn't imagine sitting any longer than this, however. One and half days seemed plenty to me.

About this time a member of my book club told me she was going to do a week-long retreat at Spirit Rock Meditation Center and I wondered, "Why would she want to do that?"

Coming Home

My favorite class in high school was entitled, "From Homer to Kazantzakis" in which we read and discussed Greek literature, learned Greek folk dances, cooked lamb on a spit, and watched the movie, *Zorba the Greek*. So, after graduating from college and planning a nine-week trip to Europe with my boyfriend, John, I made sure that Greece was on our itinerary.

We booked a charter flight to Amsterdam, arriving in the early evening. On the first night of my first trip to Europe, we walked down a street looking for cheap accommodations and ended up in the red light district. Then we were confronted in a doorway by a scruffy–looking man asking if we wanted to buy weed. Right from the start I knew this vacation would be an eye-opener.

The highlights of this early travel journey included sampling luscious chocolate éclairs at patisseries throughout Paris, attending an evening Bolshoi Ballet performance of Ravel's *Bolero* in the courtyard of the Louvre, hiking in the French Alps amidst fields of brightly colored wildflowers in August, and handing over our passports to young soldiers at a checkpoint in the former Yugoslavia and then being told that everyone had to get off the bus.

We had just crossed from Italy into Yugoslavia. We wondered if we were the cause of the entire busload of people having to get off the bus with their packages. Only later did we surmise that they were making sure the travelers were not bringing in goods that were not allowed. We were frightened that the young male officials would hold onto our passports. There was nothing for us to do except trust that all would be fine.

Eventually we all were allowed back on the bus and they handed us our passports. We were on our way to the terminal where we would ferry down the coast of Yugoslavia, stopping for a couple of nights in Dubrovnik. We stayed in the beautiful old walled part of the city and one night attended a colorful performance of traditional music and dance. During the day, we walked and explored throughout the walled city and then relaxed in the clear, warm ocean waters. The sore muscles from so much walking began to melt as I floated in the Adriatic Sea and felt the warmth of the sun on my body.

Having had this experience of Dubrovnik made the Yugoslav wars, which started in 1991, that much more real. I had walked the streets of Dubrovnik, looked in the eyes of the shopkeepers and knew that this was a real place with real people. This war zone meant something to me and I felt compassion for the people whose lives, homes and businesses were destroyed by war.

Meaning came to me in other ways on this first overseas travel experience. We continued on the ferry and eventually approached the coast of Greece. I stood on the deck and as we neared the Greek shore, tears streamed down my face. I had no idea why I was crying except that I had the feeling that I was coming home.

Coming home? I had never been to Greece before. Why would I feel that way? I don't know the answer to that question now, nor did I then. I didn't tell John about what I was experiencing, wanting to keep this a special, private experience. I do know that I loved visiting Greece. I loved the weathered faces and dark eyes of the men in the cafes as they played backgammon, smoked cigarettes and drank strong coffee; the souvlaki we bought hot off the spit from the street vendors; the olive trees that dotted the dry landscape with leaves that shimmered in the blazing sun. I especially enjoyed exploring the islands of Crete and Santorini, learning about the Minoan history and culture, exploring ruins and sitting for hours in outdoor cafes. I have not been back, and yet I know that I will return. I wonder if I will feel like I am coming home once again.

Morning Bows

References to the number 108 are found in literature, martial arts, Chinese medicine, and even in the television program, *Lost*. In Homer's *The Odyssey*, Penelope, wife of Odysseus, had 108 suitors. An official Major League baseball has 108 stitches. 1-0-8 is the emergency telephone number in India. The diameter of the sun is 108 times the diameter of the earth. And these are just a few examples of the meaning and use of the number, according to Wikipedia.

And, 108 is the number of bows we do at the Zen Center in the morning. 108 is a sacred number in many Eastern religions. Mala, the prayer beads used by many Buddhist and Hindu priests and teachers, either include 108 beads, or a divisible number of 108, of which there are many. The wearer of the mala will repeat a mantra 108 times.

Bowing practice is a way of cultivating the ability to wake up in our daily life.

The *Dharma Mirror* outlines several different forms of bowing practice. (The *Dharma Mirror* is a binder that contains detailed information on the Kwan Um School of Zen practice forms and procedures. The binder is given to Dharma Teachers in Training. The first edition of the *Dharma Mirror* took seven pages to describe various forms of bowing. The third edition describes bowing in two pages.)

> The Greeting Bow form:
> Put your hands in Hapchang. (Hands facing together and pointed up at chest level with elbows down)
> Bow slightly from the waist, about 45 degrees, keeping the hands close to the body.
> Return to standing position.
> This form of bowing is used in greeting people and also as a way to say "thank you" or "goodbye."

The Dharma Mirror also describes how to do the formal standing bow, sitting bow and full prostrations. Full prostrations are done as part of morning bows (among other times). Morning bows are done at the start of early morning meditation sessions and at retreats.

I learned how to do full prostrations by watching others do it. This is challenging to do when you are bent over on your knees. I didn't know for quite some time that the correct form is to turn your hands up when you are down on your knees with your forehead almost touching the floor.

The Zen Master generally leads the bows. We are supposed to bow at the same pace as the leader. If you are not able to do the full prostration, it is acceptable to do a full standing bow or some other variation. Full prostrations give the thigh muscles a serious workout. For those who have a regular practice of morning meditation and completing 108 bows, they gain the added bonus of staying in shape.

So what is the purpose of all this bowing? Bowing is another form of meditation, of mindfulness. Through bowing I focus my attention on the movement, on staying together with the group and the leader. It is an opportunity to notice my body, my breath and my mind. It is hard to be thinking about my to-do list when I have so much else to occupy my body and mind.

I may be thinking, "why are we doing these stupid bows? Why can't I do these correctly! She can do 108 bows, why can't I?" These questions are all opportunities for reflection.

For many years, I wouldn't count the bows as I went along. Instead I would try to watch for when the leader was doing the final bows. After 108 full prostrations, we do a half prostration and then a full standing bow. I had a hard time concentrating on counting bows. I told myself that counting wasn't necessary. Once I started doing weekend retreats, I was able to focus my mind on counting the bows. Sometimes my count would match the Zen Master and sometimes it wouldn't. I have learned that counting bows is another way of focusing my mind.

Bows are just one of the ways that Zen practice is a mirror, a reflection, of our thinking and being in the world. "Am I judging how I do bows? If so, how do I judge myself in other areas of my life? Am I challenging myself? When else do I or do I not challenge myself? Am I paying attention to what I am doing now? When else do I pay attention or not?" Morning bowing practice helps me to wake up in more ways than one.

Bowing in Japan

Prior to leaving for Japan, I had my Backroads business cards translated into Japanese and the translation printed on the back of a set of cards. This was recommended by Skye, the Backroads leader who had lived in Japan for several years and would be my partner on this research trip. Our goal was to design a bicycling vacation north of Kyoto in and around the Noto Peninsula.

I recall the first time I had the opportunity to use my new business cards. We stopped at a *ryokan* (a traditional style inn) that we were considering as an overnight lodging for the trip.

Skye spoke Japanese, so she introduced us to the innkeepers. I smiled and bowed. We were an unusual business pair being women and being from the United States. This sort of active travel trip was also unusual in Japan at that time. We knew it would take some time to explain what we had in mind and for them to accept our proposal. They looked at us skeptically and then invited us in to have tea.

We sat with them for probably two hours (as we did with several innkeepers and others on that first research trip). My role was to be the older (and presumably wiser) business partner. I didn't feel too wise not knowing Japanese. I did a lot of smiling, nodding, and bowing on that trip.

Author and Skye dining at a ryokan

What was amazing as I sat in those meetings and kept my mouth shut, was that I felt like I started to understand the conversation of Skye and the innkeepers. I could tell from the expressions of the innkeepers and their tone of voice what they were most likely saying.

"Americans want to ride a bicycle in Japan and pay money to do so?" "Why would they want to stay here rather than in a hotel with amenities that Americans are used to?" "I don't think they will like the food we serve." "We don't speak English. How will that work?"

Skye asked them to consider the idea. She told them we were just beginning to do the planning and that we would like to contact them again later. She then motioned for me to hand them my business card, as she had showed me. I held the card in both hands with the Japanese side facing the innkeeper so that she could read it. I presented the card with a slight bow and reverence. The innkeeper took the card in both hands and returned the bow.

Then as we left the inn, we bowed to each other again. We were all following the proper form.

Bowing and Kong-Ans

The Zen Master and Head Dharma Teachers sometimes were strict and sticklers for the rules. They might challenge a student's question by throwing it back at her. They also provide teachings about Zen and about why and how we sit in meditation. They insure that we serve and eat meals in the correct manner, as well as monitor whether all of the other meditation forms are followed correctly. Sometimes this is done gently and other times rather sternly.

"Interviews" are held during retreats and on Saturday mornings at Empty Gate Zen Center. This is a time when one at a time, we enter the Zen Master's room at the sound of his ringing bell. We bow at the waist as we enter the room. Then, when standing in front of the Zen Master, we move the *zafutan* (round meditation cushion) to the side and do a bow from a kneeling position. We replace the zafutan and then do another standing bow before sitting down in front of the Zen Master.

When I began to practice at Empty Gate Zen Center, I questioned all of this bowing. Why should I bow to the teacher? I must confess I did so initially with some reluctance. It was only after I matured, traveled and had more experiences that I came to understand that bowing is a sign of respect and that it is done around the world, not just at a Zen Center.

When I traveled to Japan to do research for the new Backroads trip, I was struck with how much bowing went on. These weren't full prostrations, but rather a bow at the waist. At some times it became a bit comical because of the number of bows made in quick succession, but I also realized that it was a way to honor the other person. When I have been to talks by the Dalai Lama and he bows to the crowd of thousands of people before him, he is honoring us as we honor him back. I no longer question bowing when I enter the Zen Master's room.

Bowing is also a way to honor oneself and to be fully present. When I bow at the correct times, I am acknowledging and respecting the order of things at the Zen Center. It is not too dissimilar to the established protocol in our government's Senate Chamber, for example. In yoga class, we typically bow at the end of class and say "Namaste" which means "I bow to the divine in you."

Our Zen Master often begins the interview by asking if we have any questions or whether there is something we want to talk about. Jeff entertains a wider range of question topics than many Zen teachers. However, he is a psychotherapist by training and in his day job. He knows that many people who go to a Zen Center, especially when they first start attending or return after an absence, may be doing so because of some challenge or difficulty in their life. He makes time and space for the person to talk briefly about their life, if they choose to do so. I imagine that he sees his role as Zen Master as being a leader with compassion, a teacher, and a guide.

After giving the person time to talk and ask questions about their life, about Zen, the forms or about Empty Gate, he then asks a Zen *kong-an*. This is a brief story followed by a question which is paradoxical. They are designed to help us step outside of our normal thought processes and awaken to a new way of thinking and being. Zen Master Seung Sahn, in *Dropping Ashes on the Buddha*, says Zen uses the kong-an to cut off thinking, becoming empty mind.

I might give an answer to a kong-an that meets the Zen Master's satisfaction, but I only leave the Zen Master's room when I fail to answer a kong-an "correctly." I put the word "correctly" in quotes because answering correctly is up to some interpretation by the Zen Master. For some Zen practitioners, the kong-an are a fun puzzle, for others they are frustrating. I know one person who worked on the same kong-an for 20 years.

A couple of examples of kong-an questions are "What is the meaning of 'flowing water sounds are never wet?'" "The sun in the sky shines everywhere. Why does a cloud obscure it?"

My relationship with kong-an has changed over the years. At first I thought they were mind boggling. What is going on here? These kong-ans are crazy making. Now, I just go with the flow. I do not have much attachment to getting them right. When we get a kong-an wrong, this then becomes our "homework." It becomes a tool for meditation between one interview with the Zen Master and the next. That is if you can remember the kong-an that was given to you, which I often don't.

The kong-an is just one of the tools of the Zen Master and of Zen practice. Each form that we do together—eating, chanting, working and meditating helps us on our journey of gradually attaining a clear, compassionate mind which is able to help other people.

Rain in South Africa

Christian and I stepped out of the small prop plane that landed just inside Kruger National Park in South Africa. The park only allows planes to take off and land at a couple of times each day so as not to disturb the animals too much. It was raining hard when we landed as it had been for many days prior. Staff met us at the airplane door with large umbrellas and escorted us into the small building that served as a terminal.

Prior to arriving at Kruger, we had heard that there had been heavy rains in Eastern South Africa. We had just spent a week in and near Cape Town and the wine region researching a new hiking trip for Backroads. Now we were going to conduct research in the Drakensburg Mountain area. Then we planned to check out a few game reserves to find the one we wanted to include in future trips. The weather had been beautiful, if a bit warm, in the west. It was quite a different story in this region.

We rented a car and headed out of the Park. Just as we were crossing a small bridge over a swollen stream a muscular leopard quickly crossed the road in front of us. Christian nearly jumped out of his skin. He told me he had never seen a leopard in all the weeks he had spent in Kruger National Park over the past several years. He suggested that it was because their patterns were disrupted by the heavy rains. We decided to count that as a lucky omen.

During the next couple of days we called the three game reserves we intended to check out to confirm our plans to visit them. All but Conservation Corporation's Ngala Lodge told us that due to the heavy rains, they would not be able to accommodate us. The rivers were too high to cross and that would prevent us from getting into the lodges. Ngala Lodge told us to call the day we were coming to check first, but that we should be able to make it on the dirt road. If the road was flooded at the point where it intersected with a normally dry creek bed, they suggested that we drive as fast as we could to get across. If we had a problem they would have a land rover waiting on the other side to pull us to the bank.

That sounded like an adventure. So a few days later, we were driving on a narrow dirt road with scrawny trees in the distance. First we came upon three gigantic giraffe standing in the middle of the road. I was speechless observing their majestic height and leggy bearing. We stayed back and watched them from the safety of our red car. And watched. And watched. Now we were starting to get impatient. We inched forward. They didn't move. Christian lightly honked the horn. Eventually, they sauntered off the road into the savanna, and we drove on. Our hearts were pounding. We saw other animals too, in the not too far distance: zebra, elephants, and many varieties of antelope including kudu, nyala, eland, impala, and more. I had to keep pinching myself. This is the wild. This is not a zoo park.

When we arrived at the normally dry creek bed, we were confronted with a slow-moving river. There were two land rovers on the other side. Christian gunned the motor and we went for it only to find ourselves now unmoving in the middle of the river. The land rover drivers on the other side waved to us and indicated that they would attach a cable to the front of our car and drag us across to the other bank. A man waded into the river and attached the cable, got into his land rover and slowly started to move across the river. However, our car was not moving. We realized that the cable had come unattached and we waved and yelled to the driver and finally got his attention.

He had to leave the land rover and get into the river again to attach the cable while dog paddling to stay afloat. Finally he was able to reattach the cable and the land rover jerked us forward. Again, the cable came unhooked. I noticed that our car was taking on water. I reached over the front seat to the back of the car and lifted our books and papers onto the back seat so they wouldn't get even more soaked. Now water was at our ankles. We could see that the driver and men in the second land rover were starting to panic. I wondered if there could be crocodiles in the river as I watched them in the water attaching the cable yet again.

Next they attached one land rover to the second one on the bank so that we were now in a train. The front land rover gunned its motor and slowly pulled both vehicles out of the river. I was shaking. Our car was filled with water a foot deep. "What is the rental car company going to think about this?" I wondered. I tried not to let my mind go into "what if" mode. "What could have happened to us in that river?"

We were now safely on land. We opened our car doors to let some of the accumulated water escape. We drove on to the lodge and neither Christian nor I said much. We were clearly both shaken up. When we arrived at the lodge, we were greeted warmly by the staff. A nice young man opened our car door and more water came flooding out. He looked horrified. "Sir, madame, do not worry. We will clean up your car. Please come in, we will take good care of you." And, they certainly did.

For the next two days, we went out on both early morning and dusk safari trips to see an amazing array of wild animals up close. The highlight for me, as a cat lover, was watching two cuddly leopard cubs roll around and play together as their mom looked on. I wanted to reach out and hold them, though I knew that was not a wise idea.

At one of the evening safari expeditions, a male and female lion were spotted in the headlights of our vehicle. They lumbered over to our open air land rover. We were told to stay very still and seated. If we didn't break the line of our current shape, the lions would think we were one big animal and not bother us. My heart was pounding. The huge male lion let out a booming roar. I could feel the deep, resonant sound in my solar plexus. Both lions circled our land rover swishing their thick tails and checking us out before slowly moving off into the night. Christian and I looked at each other and mouthed "wow."

Throughout our stay, besides the big cats, we saw rhinos, antelope of every variety, elephants, giraffes, zebras, hyenas, colorful birds, huge spiders, and more. I was entranced by the wildlife and felt overwhelmed by how many we saw each day. How could it become common place to see an elephant saunter by the lodge?

Because of the heavy rains, the land rover got stuck in the mud a few times. The driver and guide apologized profusely and we helped, as we could, to get the vehicle unstuck. It made the experience even more of an adventure.

In the lodge great room and in our guest rooms, the couches, bedspreads and pillows were covered in beautifully hand printed fabrics designed by local villagers. Every detail was perfect. The meals were delicious and bountiful. The staff and guides were knowledgeable and extremely service-oriented. In fact, they invited Christian and I to take a flight on their small private plane to Londolozi (In Zulu, Londolozi means protector of all living things), one of their other lodges, so that we could check it out for possible inclusion in our tour. They suggested we leave the car at Ngala while they continued to clean it and then Christian could fly back to get the car and drive out in a couple of days. As I needed to return to the office, I would fly from Londolozi to Johannesburg and then back to the United States. That sounded like a good plan to me. I had no desire to repeat the river crossing in the car and who wouldn't want to check out another luxury game reserve?

This research trip to South Africa was more than just creating a fun and exciting trip for future Backroads guests. It gave me the opportunity to learn more about South Africa, its people and their tragic history of apartheid. I read Nelson Mandela's autobiography and he has become a model for me of the power of forgiveness. Christian and I made decisions on what we would include in the trip so that our guests would also have the opportunity to experience fully and learn about its history and culture. And we were given the opportunity to practice staying calm and trusting that we would be safe.

Beginner's Mind in Daily Life

Suzuki Roshi's book, *Zen Mind, Beginner's Mind,* was one of the first Zen books I read. Truth be told, I am not sure I ever finished it the first time I picked it up. However, over the past 30 years or so, I think about it and read parts of it from time to time. What exactly is beginner's mind?

In June 2006 I started a year-long Professional Coaching Course with New Ventures West in San Francisco. I was part of a class of 20 people ranging in age from 25 – 65 from around the country as well as Puerto Rico. In this intensive course we trained to become Integral Coaches. As part of our training, we were expected to sit in meditation every day for 20-minutes. I began a regular sitting practice for the first time in my life.

Another one of our assignments was to engage in a new activity that required us to be coached, for example to learn a new musical instrument, a new sport or form of artistic expression. The idea was for us to practice "beginner's mind." What is it like to experience something for the first time? What can having a fresh perspective teach us about how we act, react, or experience our thinking?

I chose to take flamenco dance lessons. Each Saturday morning and sometimes on a Tuesday or Wednesday night also, I put on a long flowing skirt, grabbed my flamenco shoes and castanets, and practiced beginner's mind. The first half of the class was designed for beginners. However, all but one of the other students had been taking the class for several months or even years. They ranged in age from ten to 60 years old. About half-way through the hour and a half long class, more advanced students joined us.

Our teacher, Alicia Zamora, skillfully instructed the other beginner and me while also working with and demonstrating steps to the more advanced dancers.

We started with some warm up exercises and then practiced the first *copla of sevillanas* (Andalusian folk dance verse). I gave myself permission to be patient as I was learning this new dance style. I enjoyed the movements, the soulful music and the rhythms. Having danced many different styles since I was a child, my body was infused with a dance vocabulary. I was relieved that the flamenco movements did not hurt my knees or lower back, which were my weak spots. I came home from the first class energized and looked forward to the next class.

During the second class Alicia showed me the arm movements that accompanied the foot and body movements. It was now getting more complex. I continued to give myself space to learn and have fun in the class. I realized the concentration would be helpful for my brain health – moving my body, remembering sequences of movements and rhythms just might contribute to stimulating brain cells. Watching my mom suffer from Alzheimer's disease, I was keenly aware of my own brain and its lapses.

Then about a month after I started dance class, I felt frustrated.

I couldn't remember the sequence of steps once I got home so practicing was a challenge. In class, I had trouble combining the arm and body/foot patterns. It was a humbling experience. I had always been able to learn dance steps quickly. I discovered that my brain and body were not as agile at 53 years old. I wanted to be able to put it altogether as easily as I would have in the past, but that was not the case. I didn't feel like I was actually dancing. I felt like I was doing steps but not getting into the mood and moving freely to the music so that I could express the emotion of the dance.

One middle aged woman who had been taking classes longer than I told me how well I was doing. I did not share her evaluation of my competence. Taking flamenco dance class turned out to be an excellent exercise for observing beginner's mind. In the beginning, it was fun to learn something new and to watch with admiration the advanced students. I enjoyed learning a new vocabulary, how to hold the castanets, and how to assume the proud stance of a flamenco dancer. From the library, I checked out videos about flamenco so that I could learn more about the culture and music. And then, when it started to get challenging, I began to get frustrated.

I observed my critical mind. "You should be able to do this easily. Why aren't you practicing more? You can't just expect to go to class once a week and then be good at it. What is your excuse this week?" I tried to observe these thoughts and not let them take over. When else do these judgments arise?

Studying flamenco dance was also an example of how I often start a new activity with much enthusiasm and then get frustrated by how long it takes to get proficient. Am I willing to put in the sweat equity to feel a sense of mastery? I stuck with the flamenco class for six months and then decided that it had served its purpose to help me explore beginner's mind.

Five Precepts

In March 2007, I participated in a formal evening Precepts Ceremony at the Empty Gate Center. I took five precepts with two other Zen Center members and two additional people became dharma teachers in training (taking ten precepts) – including Mark.

The five precepts:
I vow to abstain from taking life.
I vow to abstain from taking things not given.
I vow to abstain from misconduct done in lust.
I vow to abstain from lying.
I vow to abstain from intoxicants, taken to induce heedlessness.

I believed and still do that I can honor these precepts for the most part. Every day, every moment, I make choices about how I live. I choose to live in harmony with these precepts or to occasionally make a conscious choice to forgo them.

On one day-long retreat I spent a fair amount of time thinking about shoes. The previous day I browsed in The Walk Shop in Berkeley. They sell shoes meant to be comfortable and many are quite expensive. I tried on a pair of mint green, soft leather flats. They were beautiful and so comfortable. And they cost a whopping $350. I didn't buy them, but the next day I found myself lusting after them as I sat in meditation. I certainly saw the irony in this situation. Finally, after one sitting period I was able to let go of the lust before it got the better of me. Would buying the shoes have been misconduct? In my mind it would have been. In someone else's, it would not.

As part of taking five precepts, Zen Master Bon Soeng chose my Buddhist name. He selected, Bo Soeng. He translated it as "Wide Nature." On the envelope of my precepts certificate Bo Soeng was translated as "Treasure Nature." What do "Wide Nature" or "Treasure Nature" mean? This is something I will ponder for my whole life, like a Zen kong-an. My current thoughts reveal:

- being open to what is
- seeing clearly what is around and in me
- appreciating "nature" in all its definitions

I must admit, I "like" my Buddhist name. Zen Master Bon Soeng would caution me to be careful of my likes and dislikes.

The certificate given to me that day includes the name and logo of our Zen school: "The Kwan Um School of Zen, Zen Master Seung Sahn, Founding Teacher." Then it has the word, "Revelation" typed above my original name and then my Buddhist name, Bo Soeng.

I puzzled over the word "revelation." Why was that typed on the certificate? What does it mean?

The American Heritage dictionary defines revelation 1. Something revealed. 3. *Theology*. A manifestation of divine will or truth.

I do feel that something has been and continues to be revealed to me through my participation in Zen.

I did not expect taking the five precepts to be a big deal. In fact, it wasn't a "big deal" at the time I took them. But, over time becoming a part of the Kwan Um School of Zen by taking the precepts has become more important to me. Something was revealed. I became part of a community, a *sangha*. I began to sit in meditation more frequently. I started to have some beginning understanding of Zen teachings.

Also on the certificate is a poem written by Zen Master Seung Sahn.

> Good and evil have no self-nature;
> "Holy" and "unholy" are empty names.
> In front of the door is the land of stillness and light.
> Spring comes; the grass grows by itself.

I read this as a cautionary poem. Just because I have taken the five precepts does not make me holier or better than anyone else. The grass grows by itself. It needs no help or assistance from me.

At the Precepts ceremony I was also given a *kasa*, an elaborately sewn brown bib, meant to symbolize the cloth of Buddha. This is worn over a short gray robe. A fellow Zen student taught me how to tie the robe. For me, putting on my robe and kasa prior to entering the dharma room symbolizes respect for the teachings and invites me into a community of practitioners.

It also comes with some responsibility to follow the precepts, to welcome newcomers to the Zen Center and to represent our

Center well through my everyday practice.

In the letter that accompanies the application to take precepts, Zen Master Soeng Hyang wrote, "Taking the five precepts means recognizing the importance of practicing, and making it part of your everyday life. It means joining a family of other people who have made the same decision, practicing with them when you can." Again, these words didn't mean that much to me when I read them initially, but they do now.

Sitting practice has become a part of my life and I do feel like I am a member of the Empty Gate Zen Center community.

Robes hanging in hallway at Empty Gate Zen Center

The Best Laid Plans

I was chosen to co-lead the first Backroads trip ever offered in Europe, a bicycle tour that led us on country roads past the grand chateaux in the Loire Valley of France. I was given this honor not because I spoke fluent French, was an ace bicycle mechanic, or was one of the most experienced leaders, but because I had done the trip research with Tom, the owner of the company, and had followed up with the planning and negotiations from the office.

The day before we were to leave for France, my more experienced co-leader, Jill, sheepishly appeared in the office. "Sue, I can't find my passport," she admitted. In surprise, I answered, "Are you sure?" While she negotiated for an emergency passport and a change of flight, I headed to France by myself on a night flight.

Arriving in the morning, I rented a car at the De Gaulle airport and drove to Belgium to pick up the rental van that we would use for the trip. The Operations Manager at Backroads had gotten a better deal renting a van in Belgium than in France. I had never been to Belgium before, not that I saw anything more than the airport where I picked up the van. For that matter, I had never driven by myself in Europe prior to this trip. I experienced quite a few "firsts" on this work trip.

At the airport in Paris, I exchanged a small amount of my own money. Jill had the Backroads traveler's checks as she was designated the "head leader." I made the drive to Belgium with very little sleep as well as very little cash. I unexpectedly had to pay a few tolls along the way and was already running low on money. I also was not thinking too clearly as I was personally running on fumes.

I did manage to find my way to the airport in Belgium and rent the van. Let me remind you that this was prior to cell phones and "Siri" guiding my way. Unlike the usual experience of renting a car, the van was not full of gas. And, I had not exchanged any money for Belgium francs, only French francs. At the gas station, I showed the service agent my French francs. In my limited French and animated sign language, I asked him to fill the tank with however much gas my francs would get me. He took my money and added gas to the tank. As I write this I wonder why I didn't hand him a credit card. But this was many years ago, and I don't recall the answer to that question. It could be that with lack of sleep I didn't think about it or it could be that Jill had the Backroads credit card and I had not brought a personal credit card.

Now I was worried that I would come upon a freeway toll prior to getting across the border with France. I was aware that worrying wasn't going to change whether a toll booth appeared so I tried to focus on driving. Fortunately, I made it across the border and exchanged more of my personal dollars at the first opportunity. I had to stop a couple of times to take brief naps on the way back to Charles De Gaulle airport to pick up Jill. I finally arrived at the airport and just as I pulled up to the outside of the baggage claim, Jill walked out the door. My timing was impeccable. I got out and gave her a hug and turned the keys over to her. This would not be the first time that I eagerly turned over car keys to a co-leader.

Jill announced, "Let's drive to the Loire Valley. I am eager to get going with all of the work we have to do." Through my tired eyes I responded, "Really?" I was looking forward to spending the night in Paris. "Okay, but only if you drive," I finally responded. On the drive south, I filled her in on my Belgium adventure, only the first of many on this trip.

Soon after arriving in the Loire Valley we discovered that the bikes that had been shipped from the United States to France had not arrived. After many telephone calls, we finally located them in a warehouse at a shipyard on the coast of France. The man on the telephone told us, "*No, ce n'est pas possible.*" He repeated several times that it was not possible to truck them to the Loire Valley *immédiatement*. We needed time to put the bikes together prior to the start of the trip. We were exhausted, and tearful and fearful. How are we going to pull off this trip?

"*Monsieur, s'il vous plaît, nous avons besoin des vélos immédiatement,*" we implored. All we could do was hope that he understood our urgency.

In the meantime we needed to drive the entire bicycle route, update the biking turn-by-turn directions, check in with each of the hotels on the route to review our rooming and dining needs, and make copies of the new directions for each guest. We had very few days to accomplish all of this.

We drove the route and each night hand wrote the corrected directions, as we did not have access to a computer. When we had completed the revised directions, we searched for a photocopier.

The only one we could find made only one copy at a time and required that we plug francs into the machine. It took hours. This all sounds so primitive now, and it was.

We were supposed to be camping during the pre-drive. However, given that we had so much work to do at night, that it was raining, and we were exhausted, we made the executive decision to get a cheap hotel for a couple of nights. The budget we were given for food was based on food prices in the United States. Jill and I stood outside a basic café and looked at the prix fixe menu one night and laughed and cried when we saw that our food budget for the entire day didn't even cover the cost of a simple pre-fixe menu.

We kept calling the first night's chateau hotel, where the bikes were to be delivered, "*Halo, monsieur, les vélos, sont-ils arrivés?* "*Pas encore*" (not yet), he always replied.

"Should we turn the trip into a walking tour?" I asked Jill. She replied, "We don't have time to research walking routes." We were tired and stressed and yet we knew we had to trust that all would work out in the end. That night Jill backed the van into one of those beautiful French stone walls. It only dented the brand new van a little bit.

After driving the entire route, finishing up the directions, and checking in with each hotel, a couple of long days later we arrived back to the trip's first hotel, a Relais & Chateaux palace. We were all ready for the guests to arrive the next day, except for the fact that we had no bikes.

And then, miraculously, a large truck pulled into the circular drive. Jill and I looked at each other and began to laugh. And then we started to pray and move very fast. We had that afternoon and the next morning to assemble the bikes with the requested pedals (toe strap or not) and handlebars (upright or not) on the right size bike for the guests on this first trip of the season and then complete a safety check of each of these bikes. We worked our butts off.

I was not a very skilled bike mechanic so Jill ended up with most of the work on the bikes. I was good at rolling the bikes across the gravel parking lot, down the hilly lawn and into the storage space next to the wine cellar in the basement of the hotel. As it began to get dark, I wheeled the bikes to the back of the hotel in full view of the elegant diners. What a surprising sight we must have been to the dinner guests as we were in shorts (not proper French attire) and disheveled from all of the work.

I remember that the hotel staff felt sorry for us and brought us out some dinner. At some point we decided that we needed to finish in the morning, and headed off to our poor woman's pension. The following night we would stay at the elegant chateau with our guests and dine in the very dining room from which we were trying to hide our presence the night before.

The next morning we arose early and headed back to the chateau. We decided that Jill would continue working on the bikes and I would pick up the guests from the train station. When I arrived back at the hotel with a vanload of guests, Jill was no longer in the driveway fixing bikes. After checking in the guests and telling them when we would gather outside to fit them to their bikes, I found Jill in our spacious room. We looked at each other and began to laugh uncontrollably. It was laughter of relief, exhaustion, and pride that we had pulled it off.

And now, we needed to pull off leading an exceptional Loire Valley vacation for our guests. We rested for a few minutes, and then went out to meet the guests and introduce them to their very special bikes. We did not tell them until the final night of the trip that our "plan B" was to run a spontaneous walking trip.

8-Day Zen Meditation Retreat

It did not begin with a big *aha* moment. The decision to sit my first 8-day meditation retreat seemed to just slip into my consciousness. It was only a year prior when I wondered why in the world anyone would choose to spend their time that way.

Mark and I were sitting at the breakfast table at the beginning of January in 2009 and we both revealed that we were thinking about doing the entire 8-day retreat. At Empty Gate Zen Center, an 8-day retreat is scheduled once per year at the end of January. On that particular morning when we mentioned the retreat, it was in casual conversation. We both just said we were thinking about it. However, now that we had verbalized our thoughts, we then started to plan how we would make that possible.

I blocked out the week on my work calendar. Then I began to plan the practical aspects of taking a week off from my normal routine. Like going on a vacation, I had to think about whether to stop the mail and newspaper, how to take care of our cat, keep the houseplants watered and notify clients that I'd be away.

Part of planning for the retreat was thinking about what

kind of accommodations I wanted during this experience. Sleeping at the Zen Center would be like indoor camping (sleeping on a pad on the floor in the dharma room or in the lounge), or I could sleep at home in my own, comfortable bed. The later would mean getting up earlier in the morning in order to be at the Zen Center by 6 am. We wouldn't get home until 10 p.m.

Just like planning a vacation, I had to decide on the level of comfort that I desired versus location. I did not have to consider price in this case, as the cost of the retreat was the same whether I slept there or not. I knew that sitting all day was going to be challenging for my body, so a good night's sleep was important. I wondered if I would be able to maintain the retreat mood if I went home at night? I weighed the pros and cons and decided to sleep at home each night, as did Mark.

We had recently adopted Sapphire, a very social cat. By our choosing to sleep at home, we could feed her in the morning and evening and give her a bit of attention. Sapphire was used to my being around during the day as my office is in the home. I spent a fair amount of time calling friends and neighbors and finally arranged for at least one person to visit her each day.

The daily retreat schedule was set, meaning I did not need to plan what I would do each day. Meals were prepared unless I volunteered to cook a particular meal for everyone. I also was not involved in selecting my fellow travelers.

There were other details of the retreat experience that I did plan. I decided that I wanted to try and keep the silence of the daily retreat as much as possible. I let friends, family, work colleagues and clients know that I would not be checking nor answering email or phone calls, though I didn't reveal to most people where or what I would be doing during that week.

Mark and I decided we would try to maintain silence on our drives to and from the Zen Center and while at home. I cancelled the newspaper and refrained from listening to the radio. I did pack my iPod in my "carry on" bag.

During the week prior to the retreat, I started packing this carry-on bag that I planned to leave at the Zen Center. I saw this as my safety net or good girl scout "be prepared" bag. In it I put extra socks, clothes for yoga class, my journal, a book, ibuprofen, toothbrush and toothpaste, water bottle, shawl, towel, and an umbrella.

I planned to go to a yoga class every other day. I knew that sitting for so long would be hard on my body and that I would need to stretch. I spent a lot of time researching yoga classes that weren't too far away from the Zen Center and that might fit the sitting schedule.

As on a vacation, sometimes we research activities or places to visit, but once we get to our destination we realize that is not what we want to do. I certainly did not anticipate this is how I would feel during the retreat. I imagined that I would relish leaving the Zen Center and having a break from the intense schedule.

I never did go to a yoga class. I never listened to my iPod nor did I read, except prior to sleep on some nights. I found that I wanted to keep silence in all respects - to limit the amount of input into my consciousness so that I could be truly present.

Sapphire did fine despite the fact that on half of the days that I had lined up visitors, they ended up not being able to come. So, just like a vacation, many of my plans either got set aside due to my own decisions once on retreat, or due to circumstances outside of my control. As we drove up to the house at night, I would often see Sapphire in the window welcoming us home. There's no place like home.

Sapphire at window

A Memorable First Trip Day in France

The first day of any trip is filled with anticipation. And the Loire Valley trip, perhaps more than others due to its being the first Backroads European trip, held much anticipation. And for Jill and me, with all that led up to this day, added further excitement. I was to drive the van on the first day and Jill would ride sweep and then we would alternate jobs.

We were perhaps 3 kilometers out from the hotel when I spotted a half dozen guests stopped beside a rock wall alongside the murky Loire River. I pulled the van over and got out. The next thing I noticed was that one of our guests was **in** the Loire River along with his red bike. It was the strangest sight. How did he get in the river? He held in his raised hand the red apple he had packed into his front bike bag as a snack for later in the day. The image seemed biblical.

The other guests and I managed to rescue our "swimmer" and his bike from the dirty river. Miraculously, he was not hurt. He was unable to explain to us just how he ended up in the river! He was a good sport and got right back on his bike, seemingly unfazed by his early morning dip. I replaced his apple and he and the others went on their way.

I sat in the van for a few moments to calm myself. Wow, another lucky break. Jill rode up to the van and I told her about what had just happened. We looked at each other and laughed.

Thirty minutes later I pulled the van to the side of the road again as two of the female guests were stopped. One was the wife of the "swimmer." She had just fallen off of her bike as her wheel had caught on the lip of the road. She gashed her knee. While she said she was fine and could keep going, I could see ligaments just barely covered by skin and knew that I needed to get her to a doctor. It was not a pretty sight.

She dutifully climbed into the van along with her new riding partner. As luck would have it, I recalled from the pre-drive seeing a Red Cross sign on a building not far from where we were. I stopped there and an older woman dressed in black cautiously opened the door. *"Madame, il y a un médecin ici?"* She pointed, *"Pas ici, allez-y toutes droites jusqu'a l'allée du son chateau."* (Not here, go straight until the driveway for his chateau.)

We pulled into the circular drive of an elegant home not far away and all three of us got out of the van. A woman in pearls and a tailored navy dress answered the door. She looked at us in our bike clothes, saw our wounded companion, and invited us to enter. The doctor was having his lunch and would be with us shortly. She directed us to his home medical office. This was a new cultural experience for us. Are there doctors in the United States who have their medical offices in their homes?

We waited quietly taking it all in. The doctor arrived, wiping food off the corner of his mouth. Fortunately, he spoke English. He helped "Cheryl" onto the examination table. I held Cheryl's hand as the doctor vigorously cleaned out the wound. I felt woozy watching this procedure so decided to sit down or risk fainting and adding to the drama.

The kind doctor stitched her up with staples and placed a bandage on her knee. He gave us directions for cleaning and bandaging the wound and a list of supplies that we should purchase. We thanked the doctor and apologized for interrupting his lunch.

Back in the van we found a pharmacy in a nearby small village, handed the supplies list to the pharmacist who returned with a small bag, and we then headed to our next hotel. By now, the other guests had arrived back at the hotel and had walked on to the mushroom caves for a visit. Cheryl wanted to go there too. I suggested that she rest, but she was not to be dissuaded. She and her husband became the models for persevering in the face of misfortune. They inspired everyone on the trip.

That night we toasted the guests and their spirit of adventure. Fortunately, the rest of the trip included only planned adventures and excitement.

You Have Got To Be Kidding

I only told a few people that I would be going on an 8-day silent Zen meditation retreat, as I didn't think others would understand or worse think I was crazy. "You are doing what? Sitting in a small room in Berkeley for 8 days and not talking? Why would you want to do that? I could never do that!"

As it turned out, even the few people that I told didn't know how to respond. I watched them search for the right words and then at a loss liken it to a vacation, perhaps to an exotic location. "Have a great time. I could use a week off right now. I'm jealous." These are some of the send-off comments I received from friends prior to going on the retreat.

I smiled and said "Thank you." Inside, I was thinking, "Yeah right, have fun. You have got to be kidding." However, I did not really know what it would be like. I had never done an 8-day retreat. The most I had sat consecutively was a day and a half. I knew that this would be different.

I surely was not thinking of it as a vacation. So why in the world would I spend eight days sitting on a cushion when I could be snorkeling in Kauai or bicycling in Provence? Some Zen retreats are at least located in beautiful mountain or ocean settings. At this retreat we would focus on our practice inside the walls of the dharma room.

One of the many questions I asked myself during the first days of the retreat was, "What am I doing here?" My back hurt. My knees hurt. My neck and shoulders hurt. By the evening sitting period I was in a lot of pain, and I had a hard time focusing on anything besides the pain.

However, after a few days of sitting, the pain became more tolerable and my mind became clearer. "What am I doing here?" receded from my mind. Over the course of the week, I realized that there actually were similarities between a vacation and a Zen retreat.

Fear

Who would have thought that I would experience fear after returning from a trip to Canada? I had traveled to several "third world" countries prior to this vacation in Alberta and had been in situations that I would never allow myself to get into at home. I had ridden on buses that looked like they had never been inspected, boats that were overcrowded, and small planes high in the Himalayan Mountains making landings on airstrips that were very short.

In 1992, I signed up for what was billed as a healthy hiking vacation in Alberta, Canada. The idea was that we stayed all week in a comfortable lodge, setting goals at the beginning of the week for diet, exercise, or some other area of our life. We went on daily hikes in the mountains, ate healthy, vegetarian food, drank no coffee, and were treated to a daily massage.

On the 5th day of the trip it was raining as we set out. Our group was divided between those who chose the more vigorous hike who rode in the jeep and the majority of us in the van who would do a more moderate hike led by the owner of this small hiking adventure company.

We drove along narrow dirt roads to the start of our hike, as we had each day. The vigorous hike led us through pine forests and up and down slippery muddy trails. We wore our matching yellow rain pants and jackets that kept us relatively dry during the rainy parts of the hike. At the end of the day, we warmed up a bit in a cabin at the trailhead before climbing back into the van.

As we headed down the mountain, I experienced the van moving in slow motion—front right tire driving off the edge of the dirt road, the back right tire and then the van falling off the road into the forest. We landed upside down. The windows of the van broke with the impact, and the van's horn was blaring. We called out to each other to check if we were each okay. Everyone appeared to be so though our leader did not answer. We were afraid to move for fear we would cause the van to slide or even roll down the slope.

As luck would have it, another vehicle had not been too far behind us and had seen us go off the road. They stopped, let one person out to check on us as the other drove down the mountain to get help. A woman appeared and told us we were okay. She said that the van was wedged between two trees and that she was going to help us get out one by one. Calmly, we each slithered out a broken window and climbed up the steep slope to the road. Each hiker helped the next as we got out of the van safely.

The driver, our leader, seemed to be in shock. She had a bump on her head and did not say anything. We helped her up the slope and laid her down on the road. Soon, the Canadian mounted police arrived and they took us all to a hospital to be checked out. We were all okay, amazingly. Our trip leader was kept longer at the hospital than the rest of us, but she was released that evening.

That night we talked about what could have happened. We all

felt a sense of relief and wonder. Our fellow hikers who were not in the van and our masseuses felt just as much fear and relief as we did. And the next day, with a rented van, we went out hiking again. Our leader took the day off, and we were happy that she did.

This event changed my life for many years. When I was a passenger in a car, I felt a loss of control and would put on the brake, hold onto the dash and shout, "watch out" and otherwise bother the driver of the vehicle. These actions especially annoyed Mark when he was driving. I felt what seemed like real fear. I was afraid we were going to get in a car accident. For many years, I felt that my eventual death would be by car accident.

These fears have dissipated over time, though I still sometimes overreact as a passenger. Sometimes if I catch myself being jumpy in the car, I will close my eyes and focus on my breath. I try to notice what is going on and relax my thoughts and body. I tell myself to "be here now" as Ram Dass titled his classic book. Tensing my body is not going to help the person driving the vehicle nor is it going to help me.

Calculating

Prior to the first day of the retreat, I wrote down the entire day's schedule on a piece of paper. I wanted to know exactly what I was getting myself into.

Retreat Schedule

6:00	108 bows
6:30–6:50	morning bell chant
6:50–8:00	two 30-minute sitting periods with 10-minute walking meditation in between
8:10	formal breakfast
8:40–9:40	work period
9:40–10:00	break
10:00–12:30	four 30-minute sitting periods with 10-minute walking meditation in between
12:40	formal lunch
1:00–2:00	break
2:00–4:30	four 30-minute sitting periods with 10-minute walking meditation in between

4:30–5:30	break
5:30	formal dinner
6:00–6:30	break
6:30–7:30	chanting
7:30–9:20	three 30-minute sitting periods with 10-minute walking meditation in between
9:20–9:30	chanting

The schedule was the same from day 2 through day 8, with days 1 and 9 being shorter than the above schedule. The evenings of day 6 and day 8 were slightly different too. Every other day we had a private interview with Zen Master Bon Soeng.

I calculated that this schedule included a total of thirteen 30-minute sitting periods, or 390 minutes or six hours and thirty minutes of sitting per day. I had a hard time imagining how I was going to sit for that long. I asked myself, "Can I do it? Will I be able to keep it up for the entire retreat?" I knew that I had outs. I could take longer breaks and I could go for walks. I could end the retreat early. I had options.

Just like prior to a vacation, I was anticipating what the experience might be like. I felt some trepidation and fear about this Zen retreat.

At some point, I had to trust that I had prepared myself as best as I could and had to jump into the experience.

On the first morning of the retreat, "Robert," a dharma teacher who was the retreat leader, informed us that those of us who were sitting the entire retreat should sign up most every day on the schedule sheet hanging from the refrigerator in the kitchen to either cook a meal or clean up in the kitchen. During the first sitting period, I calculated that if I signed up to make several meals, I would be able to prepare the meals during at least one or two of the sitting periods. This would be a break from sitting that seemed welcome to me. So, I signed up to make dinner that first night and the next night. I also cooked breakfast and two more dinners during the course of the retreat.

During the first two days I spent a fair amount of time during the meditation periods planning and calculating the meals. "How many people are in the room? Will they all be here for dinner? How much rice do I need to cook? What should I make?" After spending time with this kind of thinking the first two days, I decided that I needed to take a break from cooking so that perhaps I could quiet my mind from all this mind meal preparation.

During the first couple of days I was also thinking about my work. I calculated how many clients I needed each month in order to make a certain amount of income. I amazed myself how long it took to make these calculations in my mind without a piece of paper or my computer. I remembered that I needed to remind my brother to make an appointment for our dad with his accountant to do his taxes. I was thinking about lots of small and tedious things during those first few sitting periods. I was also in a lot of physical pain.

As I prepared dinner the first night, I enjoyed the process of choosing which vegetables to cook and deciding how to prepare them. It being the first night of the retreat, the vegetables were very fresh. I had grocery shopped the day before so I knew that beautiful bunches of rainbow chard were available. I decided to use the chard along with other vegetables, stir fry tofu and onions to serve along with brown rice and a green salad. I am not in the habit of cooking for eleven people so I was concerned that I was making enough food. I recall asking someone who wandered into the kitchen if she thought it was enough. I was conscious that I was breaking silence. I felt that I needed confirmation that what I was doing was okay.

I marveled at the beauty of the chard as I chopped several bunches. Then I thought to myself, "I am a cooking goddess." Now this was a strange thought for me. I do not think of myself as a goddess. My mom was the one in our family who had a library full of books on goddesses. I also mused that that is surely a "big I" thought. I am chopping vegetables. No need to put a label on it or me.

When Robert read the temple rules at the beginning of the retreat, the instructions say to not take pleasure in our food. My first thought was that our founding teacher, Zen Master Seung Sahn, surely had not spent much time in the gourmet ghetto of Berkeley. Why not take pleasure in our food? I understand the idea of not becoming obsessed with food and not over eating. But I don't understand the idea of not taking pleasure in food. I decided that I would ask Jeff about this at my first interview.

> *On Eating:*
> An eminent teacher said, "A day without work is a
>   day without eating."
> There are two kinds of work: inside work and
>   outside work. Inside work is keeping clear mind.
>   Outside work is cutting off selfish desires and
>   helping others.
> First work, then eat.
> Eat in silence. Do not make unnecessary noise.

THE KEY TO THE CASTLE

While eating, attend only to yourself. Do not be concerned with the actions of others.

Accept what is served with gratitude. Do not cling to your likes and dislikes.

Do not seek satisfaction in eating. Eat only to support yourself in your practice.

Though you may eat good food all your life, your body will die.

The Great Way is not difficult.
Simply cut off all thought of good and bad.
Salt is salty.
Sugar is sweet.

Perseverance in Patagonia

One of my research trip assignments for Backroads was to design a new hiking vacation in Patagonia, in southern Chile and Argentina. I had done the office research, investigating "must see" places to visit and luxury accommodations in the region. I was to meet a Backroads trip leader, "Dan," in Santiago, Chile and we would conduct the research together. He had just finished leading trips in the Lakes Region of these two countries and spoke fluent Spanish.

I arrived in Santiago in the morning after 20 hours of flights. I picked up a rental car and asked for directions to the modest hotel where Dan had spent the previous night. I thought I understood the rental agent's directions even with my elementary knowledge of Spanish. I headed out and after not too long realized that I was not headed in the right direction. I drove back to the airport to start over.

Eventually I was on what appeared to be the road to downtown during the morning rush hour. Several lanes of traffic headed in the direction I was traveling, yet none of the vehicles observed actual lanes. With so many buses on the road it was impossible for me to read the small street signs. I was sweating and fear was rising.

How would I find the street I was looking for? I didn't even have a detailed map of Santiago. And back then, GPS and cell phones were not part of my travel bag.

I finally made my way over to the far right side of the street so I could at least turn off the main drag. I made an arbitrary decision to turn right on a small street. How did I know that this was in the vicinity of Dan's small hotel?

Unbelievably, within a few blocks, I spotted the street name where Dan's hotel was located. And as I pulled up in front, Dan happened to be on the street heading out to get breakfast. Boy, was I glad to see him. I handed him the keys and said, "Please, will you drive during the rest of this research trip?" He was more than happy to comply.

Sitting in my office in Berkeley the week prior to this trip, I hadn't thought about what it would be like to navigate to the hotel after landing in Santiago with little sleep and much traffic. After I rented the car, it started to dawn on me that this could be challenging. Then, as I drove into town in a dazed state, I wondered if I would be able to find Dan. I knew that I had no choice but to persevere, so that is what I did.

Dan went off to get breakfast and I went to the room to chill. I made it. I was safe. I did it!

Several days later, as Dan and I drove along the deserted and barren roads in Southern Patagonia, we occasionally saw another car along the side of the road with a flat tire. Dan told me that sometimes rental cars didn't have a spare tire or the spare would be flat. I thought to myself, we did not check the spare when we rented our car.

In fact, we were just happy to even be able to get a car. We had planned to head out on the Patagonia portion of our research trip on Sunday. The place where we were to rent our car was closed. The next day we went to the "agency" in this small Chilean town to pick up the car, and they told us that they didn't have any. We told them that we had reserved a car. After much back and forth conversation, we started to get the picture that they did not want to rent a car to us because we planned to drive into Argentina. More talk. We then had to go to the home of the Mayor. Eventually, we were able to rent a car and headed off many hours later.

When we got to the border between Chile and Argentina, we navigated a complicated process of stopping at the Chilean border and giving them our stamped letter of permission to drive across the border, along with our passports. Then we drove through the no-man's land of 50 meters or so. We parked and entered the Argentina border check cottage where we went through the same procedure. We felt like we were criminals and had something to hide. It was scary for seemingly no apparent reason.

We finally made it across the border and breathed a sigh of relief. Fast forward a couple of days and we were driving on rough road through the steppe-like plains headed towards Los Glaciares National Park.

Next thing we knew, we heard a pop and realized that a tire had blown out. We looked at each other with panic in our eyes. We were both thinking the same thing. Do we have a spare? Does the spare have air in it? Do we have a jack? We were in the middle of nowhere. The wind was fierce. Dan started to swear loudly.

We got out and I decided to let Dan handle this. Not that I had much experience in tire changing anyway. He opened up the trunk and looked around. He pulled out the spare. Then he started to look for the jack and began to swear more loudly. He threw the spare on the road. Now I started to worry. I asked Dan to calm down. He found the jack, and I went to get the spare lying near the side of the road. As the cold wind blew, he managed to get the new tire on the car and we eventually headed off. Phew. That was stressful. We drove on in silence.

In the early 80's, I lived for a year with my older brother, Robert, in Mill Valley, California. Sometimes on Sunday mornings we drove to Green Gulch Zen Center near Muir Beach for their community meditation practice and dharma talk. On one occasion a visiting monk gave the dharma talk. He talked about leaving Viet Nam on a boat and using his practice of meditation to remain calm and to be a comfort to the other refugees on the boat.

When I listened to this quiet monk talk, I felt a special presence emanating from him. Only many years later did I realize that this soft spoken monk was Thich Nhat Hanh, who later wrote many books on Zen and has shared his teachings worldwide. I remember he also talked about doing our everyday tasks with care. When we wash dishes, pretend that we are washing the baby Buddha.

I thought about Thich Nhat Hanh's teachings as I tried to remain calm on a deserted road in Patagonia with a stressed out *compadre*. I practiced being the calm person on the boat, or in this case on the windswept plains of Argentina and on the traffic filled streets of Santiago, Chile.

Icebergs in Patagonia

Routine

Mark missed the first day of the Zen retreat because he had (or chose) to go to work, so on Saturday, he and I began our retreat routine. He got up a bit earlier than me, as is usually the case, and took a shower and made coffee. I then took my shower. One of us fed Sapphire and cleaned out her litter box. Then we headed out the door. We made it in time for bows each morning at 6 a.m., but not always early enough for Mark to hit the *moktak* (a wooden percussion instrument in the shape of a fish) announcing it was five minutes prior to bows starting.

The evening routine included feeding Sapphire and sometimes ourselves a snack. I took another shower to warm up as I was often cold sitting in the dharma room. The shower also helped to relax my tired muscles. We silently cuddled with each other and with Sapphire.

During the retreat we also had a routine. The entire day was mapped out from 6 a.m. – 9:30 p.m. This allowed us to know what to expect and to not have to make decisions or plans. It eliminated some of the day to day, moment to moment decisions we constantly have to make in a normal day.

Structure and routine are also a part of certain types of vacations. On Backroads trips—one of the reasons people like them so much—everything is planned. The accommodations, meals, trip leaders, logistics of travel, and special events are all taken care of. The guests are free to wander off on a path that pleases them, make connections with the locals and enjoy the company of their new friends on the trip.

When I went on a trek in Nepal, my friend Lisa and our Sherpa guide had planned most everything. I just needed to get up and put one foot in front of the other. It left me free to notice what was in front of me, listen to the raging rivers, observe the prayer flags flapping in the breeze, enjoy the nightly dinner of daal, and observe my reactions and thoughts, including my pain, as we hiked into higher and higher elevations.

Routine at the Zen retreat and on a vacation provided the structure from which we were free to follow our own thoughts, breath and path.

Assumptions in Bali

When I travel I love to observe how people live. What is the style of their homes? What are their family and community traditions? How and what do they eat? What are their traditional music and dance styles? What are their ways of communicating? What are their religious or spiritual practices? I try to make sense of what I am seeing. Often though, if I don't have a local interpreter, I am sure that I make assumptions that are not based on reality.

I had lunch with a young Balinese man that I had met a few days prior. We had just made a pilgrimage to Pura Besakih, mother temple of Bali, to observe a festival. We traveled there on his small motorbike and I clung to him as we switch-backed up Gunung Agung volcano. White, yellow and red umbrellas and streams of fabric adorned the temple grounds. Bamboo structures and weavings and all variety of decorations crowded the temple. Petite and graceful women streamed into the temple grounds wrapped in their finest cloth, blouses, sashes and headdresses. Men too wore fabric tied in a particular way around their body and on their heads they wore a headdress, an *udeng*, tied with the perfect peak.

ASSUMPTIONS IN BALI

The women balanced on their heads elaborate offerings of colorful fruit, flowers, and rice. I observed an abundance of ritual, beauty, chaos, conformity and symbolism that was a mystery to me. I had questions about what was going on and what it meant.

Balinese Temple Festival

Back in the town of Ubud, I suggested to my companion that we go to a café for *nasi goring*, a vegetable and rice dish that I loved. As we ate, my companion didn't say a word. I tried to make conversation. I wanted to talk about what we had just seen. I began to wonder if he was upset with me or bored with my company. Finally I asked him why he wasn't talking. He shared that Balinese prefer to eat when they are eating and save talk for another time. I was glad that I had checked this out with him so as not to continue with my incorrect assumptions.

Assumptions on a Zen Retreat

On the first night of the retreat I sat down on my cushion, relieved that I had completed dinner preparations on time. I had to make sure that each element of the dinner was ready by 5:30 p.m. In addition to the food, there are two condiment trays that include soy sauce, *kimchi* (a Korean condiment of pickled cabbage that is quite spicy), salt and pepper shakers, sunflower seeds and perhaps sesame seeds, and any other condiments for that particular dinner, such as grated cheese. And I needed to make sure that I had the correct serving spoons for each dish.

Then there are the accoutrements used in the ritual and cleaning process of our individual eating bowls. These include two plastic pitchers filled with filtered water, two teakettles of water that have been boiled and tea bags added (try not to have the water too hot by the time dinner starts), and a special empty serving bowl that is used at the end of the meal.

I was happy to finally sit down to eat after having spent the last couple of hours in the kitchen on my feet chopping, cooking, and to be frank, worrying. "Did I prepare enough food? Will the rice be done on time? Should I cook the tofu with the vegetables or keep it separate in case someone doesn't like tofu?"

I served myself dinner and all of a sudden my eyes were burning. Tears formed in the corners of my eyes. I didn't have a tissue in my pocket and I needed to blow my nose. I dabbed at my eyes and nose with the yellow washcloth used for drying our bowls. I had not yet made the connection that the washcloth shouldn't be used to wipe one's soiled hands let alone one's nose. I hadn't yet realized that it was not a napkin. Why didn't we have a napkin anyway? How did other people keep their fingers dry and clean while they ate? "Linda," sitting next to me, wordlessly handed me a tissue and I blew my nose.

Then I thought, I just made dinner and my fellow retreat participants may be wondering if I have a cold. Then I thought, or they may think that I am crying. I am crying, but they are not tears of sadness or happiness. I don't really know why I have tears, other than that my eyes are burning.

After dinner I went to the bathroom. I took off my glasses and saw why I had been crying. I had onion juice on my glasses. My eyes had been irritated by onion juice. I had to laugh. I am sure that no one in the room would have assumed that was why I was crying. On the other hand, maybe no one was paying any attention to me besides Linda who was sitting closest to me.

On another occasion during the retreat I started laughing, quite hysterically, during a meal. Mark's cushion was at the front of the room, as he was the moktak master during the retreat. (The moktak master is the person who hits the moktak five minutes before practice to call everyone to the Dharma room. He also hits the moktak to keep rhythm for the chants.)

One night during dinner, he knocked over his bowl of rice and vegetables. We both started laughing. Now ordinarily I don't laugh when he or anyone else spills something, but the meals during a retreat are formal and quite serious. And, I was having trouble at this point in the retreat with the eating style. At first we exchanged glances and then started giggling. Then I couldn't stop laughing. My mind recalled when I was a little girl and my family would go to the high holy days services at the temple. Sometimes my grandmother and I would get the giggles and not be able to stop. So by now, this was my own private joke. I was both enjoying it and also trying desperately to stop the laughter so as not to disturb the others.

The next day during a break, one of the other women on the retreat broke silence and explained to me that when she did her first silent solo retreat, she cried nonstop for three days. I looked at her quizzically wondering why she was telling me this. She referenced my crying at dinner the night before. I shared with her that I had been laughing, not crying.

A Scorpion in My Shorts

I was in the bathroom getting ready to start a new day of the Backroads bicycle trip in Baja. I showered then slipped on my bicycle shorts. I felt a sting on my behind. What was that? I pulled down my shorts and out ran a small black insect. I screamed.

I quickly wrapped a towel around my waist and called for the tour leaders to come look. I was sharing a room with them as I was a staff "guest" on the trip, and we had not booked an extra room for me. The leaders quickly came in and identified it as a scorpion. I asked them if I should be concerned. They looked at each other and said they didn't think so. It was small. I should just monitor how I felt during the day.

As it turned out, there were three doctors on that Baja bicycle trip. After breakfast I quietly went up to each one individually to ask them what they knew about scorpion bites. None of them had any experience with scorpions, but didn't think I needed to worry. So, since I was feeling fine, just a bit itchy where I had been bit, I got on my bike and didn't think much about it.

I had a good day of riding and joined one of the guests to explore a small town and have a snack before heading to our next inn along the coast. Consequently, I did not get to the room until the late afternoon. It turns out that the trip leaders were worried about me. They imagined that I was lying in a ditch somewhere due to the early morning scorpion bite. They had even gone out in the van to look for me after most of the other guests had arrived at the inn. They were quite relieved when I walked into the room oblivious of their concern.

I asked them what all the fuss was about. They had decided between them that a small scorpion was worse and that its venom could be dangerous. I am not sure how or why they decided this, but they did. In their minds I was in danger. In my mind I was fine.

Because I didn't know anything about scorpions, I chose not to worry. The leaders knew just enough to be concerned. Plus, they were in roles of responsibility for the guests on their trip. I told them that I appreciated their concern and assured them that I was doing quite well.

We may be in the same room with someone and our understanding of a situation will be quite different based on our prior experience or on our thinking. For example, one parent may spend the day worried about their child's first fishing trip on a boat with a family friend. Will he get sea sick? Will he catch a fish? Will the weather cooperate? The other parent may not be concerned about the child at all during the day. He might remember his own first day of fishing with fond memories and not be thinking about any of the concerns that are occupying his spouse's mind. They are having completely different days and their responses to their child might be quite different at the end of the day.

Through mindfulness practice I have been able to have just a bit more control over my thoughts. Now I am more often able to notice my thinking and then to decide whether I want to continue those thoughts, change them or let them go altogether. It has given me more of a sense of control and peace. My thoughts are not controlling me; I am shaping or directing my thoughts. The scorpion is in my shorts and only in my shorts. It bit my behind but not my mind.

Thinking, Thinking, Thinking

As I walked into the first retreat interview, I had a lot on my mind from all of my thinking during the first day and a half of sitting in meditation. After the requisite bows to the Zen Master, he asked how the retreat was going for me and if I had any questions.

I shared with him that I was in a lot of pain from sitting. I told him, "Sitting for so long at a retreat is like torture. Many of us are clearly in pain, both physical and emotional, and sleep deprived. I'm glad you are a psychotherapist because I imagine that someone could have a nervous breakdown."

Jeff responded, "Pain and lack of sleep can reveal our true nature. They may break down our barriers."

In reality, I did not notice anyone at this retreat having a breakdown.

I continued with my list of questions including, "Is there room for humor or spontaneity at a Zen retreat? It all seems so serious."

He answered, "In our individual practices there is room for humor and spontaneity. I have seen in past retreats that sometimes humor comes out spontaneously."

During formal meals, a woven mat is placed on the floor in the center of the dharma room. The pots, bowls of food, water pitchers and tea kettles are placed in a particular order and arrangement on the mats. I watched dharma teachers nonverbally correct the form by getting up and moving a spoon to a different angle in a pot. As I sat in the dharma room I wondered, "Is all this necessary? What is the purpose of making sure that the pot handles are facing in a particular direction? What am I to learn from the forms? What am I to learn about my concern about this?"

I asked Jeff, "What is up with all of the rules and structure during the meals? It is not even clear to me what the rules are. How can we do it 'right' if we don't know what we're supposed to do?" I went on, "I am concerned that people who attend retreats are learning to be rigid and lack spontaneity. I worry that some people might take the retreat forms into their daily lives and expect themselves and others to do things in a rigid, prescribed fashion."

When I finished my explosion of questions and opinions, Zen Master Bon Soeng said calmly, "The procedures for meals are outlined in the *Dharma Mirror*."

"But what about those of us who are not Dharma Teachers in Training and haven't been given this binder?" Zen Master shared that there are copies of the binder in the bookcase in the lounge.

It seemed that if this was something that I really wanted to know, then I needed to take the initiative to seek out the answers. I could pull the binder off the shelf and read about the retreat forms. I brought up these questions with Jeff in my first interview, but never took the next step to find out the answers. Was this laziness or did the answers cease to be as important as the retreat progressed?

In one humorous moment later in the retreat, Mark (who had been corrected a few times by Linda in his placement of the plastic honey bears on the trays), discreetly placed small written post-it notes on the backs of the honey bears and placed them lying face down on the trays. The post-it notes read, "Do not disturb honey bear bowing practice."

Linda didn't notice the notes on the honey bears until the trays were brought back into the kitchen after the meal. She (and I) got a chuckle from the joke.

I suppose most importantly during that first interview I told Zen Master Bon Soeng, "I don't know why I am at this retreat. I am in a lot of pain and clearly I am doing a lot of questioning and mindless thinking. Is this what I am supposed to be doing? Why am I subjecting myself to this pain?"

He listened to my questions and concerns and then gave me a kong-an to read and answer. When I wasn't able to answer the kong-an correctly, he dismissed me.

When Plans Go Awry

We were the four *didi's* ("older sisters" in the Nepali language) and we looked at each other and said the phrase that became our mantra, "*ke garne?*" ("what to do?", or "oh well, things happen," accompanied by a shrug of the shoulders). We were in Bangkok on a planned one-night layover on our way to Nepal for a trek and cultural adventure.

The next morning, when we returned to the check-in gate at the airport, we were told our flight had been cancelled and that we should come back the next morning. Later, we discovered that the King of Nepal borrowed our Royal Nepal Airlines jet to take a trip to Denmark.

This month-long adventure began with an invitation from a friend of a friend to join her on a trek in Nepal. Lisa had trekked in Nepal several times before and had made friends with a Sherpa guide who arranged for porters and a cook and who handled all of the logistics and planning on the Nepal side. Lisa lined up the people who would join her. She also chose the Langtang region for our trek, where we would stay in Kathmandu and took care of lots of other details.

Lisa gave us extensive information ahead of time: a preliminary equipment list, with a comment section that explained the necessity of some of the items on the list; medical notes that included what to put in our individual first aid kits as well as other notes on passports, visas, and evacuation insurance. Then she followed up with an immunization and miscellaneous notes handout along with a 7-page printout from a book that described a medical kit for trekking. And then "Final Notes" sent four weeks before take-off. This was in 1989, prior to email, so these detailed documents were mailed or hand delivered.

Those of us who lived near Berkeley also took Nepali language lessons with Lisa's teacher. Prior to leaving I had checked off everything on the list that Lisa had provided to us, learned several Nepali words and phrases, read books on Nepal and about trekking and talked with others who had been to Nepal. I felt well prepared, excited and a bit apprehensive about this journey.

I also had questions. How will my knees hold up? What will it be like to travel with this group of people? How will I feel watching porters carry my duffel bag while I only carry a day pack? How will my body react to hiking in the high elevations?

Our flight left from San Francisco on October 21, 1989. The Loma Prieta earthquake hit the San Francisco Bay Area on October 17. The 6.9 magnitude earthquake shook us all up. I wondered if I should go on the trip as planned. On our layover in the Tokyo airport, we watched on a TV screen as a man was pulled from his car from under the wreckage of the Bay Bridge four days after the quake hit. Again, I questioned whether I should be heading out on a vacation when so many people were suffering from losing their loved ones and homes. We stood silently watching the TV screen, and then our flight was called and we got on the plane.

So there we were in Bangkok where the temperature was 90 degrees and 90% humidity. We had carefully packed for a trek in Nepal with hiking boots, one long skirt, one pair of long pants, a couple of t-shirts, long underwear, a wool sweater, down jacket and a few other items of clothing that were **not** appropriate for walking the paved, busy streets of Bangkok.

Lisa was the only one of us who had ever been to Bangkok at that time, so she was our guide as we tried to make the best of our surprise layover. Each day we would either go to the airport to be turned away or call several times a day to find out if our flight would be leaving that day. This made it more challenging to be fully immersed in Bangkok and present to explore its wonders. We walked single file and quickly through the busy streets. What a sight we must have been in our long skirts and boots and sweat dripping from every pore.

We visited the magnificent Grand Palace that held the Temple of the Emerald Buddha and Wat Po with the enormous Reclining Buddha. I had never seen Buddha statues before except in museums nor such ornate architecture with gleaming gold and jewels shimmering in the intense sunlight. One day we trekked to the elegant Regent Hotel because Lisa thought that would be an easier place from which to make a telephone call to Kathmandu. She wanted to call a contact with a telephone who could let our Sherpa guide know where we were and that we would need to postpone the start of the trek. The call wouldn't go through but we did end up having formal afternoon tea in the ornate dining room. Once again we felt conspicuous in our trekking costumes as the string quartet played from the balcony and the trim waiters in their white suits and gloves served us dainty cucumber sandwiches and hot jasmine tea.

Finally, we were told that our flight would depart the next morning. Our one-night layover had become four nights. As we waited in our drab hotel lobby for the bus that would take us to the airport, more and more people filled the lobby, including a large group of Japanese students. The bus was an hour late. "Would we all fit in it? Would we ever leave Bangkok?" We fretted as we waited for the bus. Fortunately two buses were sent for us and we all made it to the airport.

There were quite a few Nepalis on the flight. I noticed how they wore many layers of clothes and that they seemed to like jeans jackets. I imagined that they had bought these clothes in Bangkok to take home to give to their family members or perhaps to sell. As I mused about the people on the plane, I glanced out the window and was treated to my first views of the magnificent Himalayan mountain range, the tallest mountains on earth. Finally, we were about to land in Nepal.

Like a meditation retreat, most of the details of this trip to Nepal were planned for me. However, already I experienced surprises and opportunities to pay attention to my mind and body and to trust that all would be fine when events did not go as planned.

A Good Day To Die

On our third day in Nepal, we were ready to depart Kathmandu for the start of our trek in the Langtang region. The rickety bus arrived at the Hotel Nook right on time at 8 a.m. As our duffel bags were being loaded onto the bus, I noticed the driver and a couple of the Nepali porters kneeling on the ground and looking underneath the bus. The fact that they ended up jump-starting the bus should have been a sign of things to come; however, we were excited to begin this phase of our journey and we didn't think much about it.

We climbed aboard along with our porters, cooks, and guides. We didn't have to travel too far out of Kathmandu before we started our ascent along switch-backed narrow roads. I began to feel *waak waak laagyo* (nauseous) but I tried to switch my attention to the beauty around me – the terraces of rice fields and wheat.

The small jangling bus slowly made its way up the curving road. The next thing we knew, the driver crashed, albeit gently, into the rock wall on the other side of the narrow road. The good part of this was that we were going slowly and no one got hurt, and that he crashed against the mountain rather than taking us down the steep slope to our right. The puzzling thing was why did this happen? We surmised that the brakes were not working. Now the front of the bus was dented and the front wheels were stuck in a narrow ditch.

For the next hour the skinny porters, wearing flip flop sandals or barefoot, rocked the bus back and forth to try and get it unstuck as we looked on. Our guide, Ang Kami, would not allow us to help. At one point a small pickup truck drove by and the driver and his passenger were reluctantly recruited to help. They attached a rope between the truck and the bumper of the bus and slowly pulled forward. The rope quickly broke and the pickup truck and its driver took off without looking back. After much effort, the porters managed to push the bus out of the ditch. Now what?

We all got back on the bus. What were our choices? We were not far from the town of Trisuli. Ang Kami told us that the bus would be looked at in this small town. He bought us a lunch of *daal baat tarkaari* (rice, lentils and vegetables) as the bus sat outside the small "café." We did not actually witness anyone doing anything to the bus (other than looking under the hood), but amazingly, we all jumped back on after lunch.

Now we were really climbing up a steep, narrow, winding road. The bus driver drove very slowly and tested the brakes frequently. I was scared. The drop offs on either side of the road were steeper than I had ever experienced. My fellow trekkers and I called it the psycho bus ride from hell. "What ifs" occupied my mind, and I created elaborate disaster movies in my head.

And then, we turned a curve and before us were the Himalayas. Tall, majestic, snow-covered peaks created a new picture for my thoughts. It was breathtaking. This was what I had been waiting for in the many months of planning, after our Bangkok pause, and the preparation days in Kathmandu. We were finally seeing the mythic Himalayas.

I said to myself, "Today is a good day to die."

Himalayan Peak

Then it started to get dark. Now we wondered if the lights on the bus would work. The road was so narrow that if another bus happened to be coming the other way, protocol required that our bus back down the hill to a place where the other bus could pass us. The lights did work and the brakes did hold as the driver made his delicate maneuvers. We arrived at 8 p.m. in Dhunche, exhausted and happy to be alive.

My fellow trekkers and I stood around a small field just above the village. This would be our home for the night. We were all dazed and relieved to be on solid ground. The porters quickly assembled our tents and the cook spread out a tarp and set to making our dinner.

Now a moral dilemma arose. We surmised as we ate our delicious dinner of daal baat tarkaari that the bus would be taken back down the hill the next morning with a load of travelers that had just completed their trek. Do we tell them that the bus may have problems?

Ang Kami was quietly furious about the bus. Lisa told us later in the trip that he had written a letter to his brother back in Kathmandu. Ang Kami asked a traveler on the bus trip back to Kathmandu to take the letter to his brother. He instructed his brother to make a complaint to the bus owner. I thought about how I would feel if I were the guide responsible for this busload of people.

In the end, I don't think anyone in our group said anything to the travelers. I know that I did not. I reasoned that we had made it up the mountain so they would likely make it down. If we told them, then they might worry the whole trip back to Kathmandu. Or, they would need to decide whether to wait for another bus to come get them. When would that be possible? Communication was not easy in Nepal in 1989.

Now when I think about this, what if something had happened to them on the bus ride? What would I have felt then?

On the harrowing journey up to the mountains, we did not freak out. As the day unfolded, our newly formed group bonded and we made jokes about our circumstances. We chose to keep most of our thoughts and fears to ourselves so as not to compound them. We realized that there just wasn't much that we could do about the situation, so we accepted it. This often feels easier to do on vacation than it does at home. On the Zen retreat it took me several days to stop critiquing the chanting and the formal eating forms and just do them.

Space in the Dharma Room

In the dharma room, those of us who sat the entire 8-day retreat had our own space – our cushion or chair. "Frank," who has back problems, set up an area at the back of the room with a long mat and a triangular block to put under his knees. "Claire" sat in a chair. I too sat in a chair for part of each day. Some people in the room sat only on their cushion. They didn't need to vary their cushions over the course of the day or eight days. They were able to sit very still and quiet, with little or no movement on their cushion and without taking up much space.

I felt like I took up a lot of space. I varied the number and types of cushions that I sat on throughout the day. I brought small pillows from home that I folded and put under each knee. Or, when I sat in the chair, I tried different pillow configurations behind my back, under my feet, under my seat. Just like Goldilocks and the three bears, I was searching for just the right combination to ease my pain. During evening chanting, one of the chants includes bows. So then I had to either move my chair out of the way or use the cushion catty-corner to my space, if no one else was sitting there. I wondered if anyone cared that I took up two spaces. Or did they even notice? Maybe I was concerned about this for nothing.

I wondered if I were to do an even longer retreat whether I would get used to sitting on the cushion and then not need to sit in a chair. Or, would my knees get even more sore and would I need to sit in a chair all of the time? I guess I won't find that out unless I do a longer retreat. Kwan Sahn Sunim, former resident monk (and now Jason Quinn), told me one night after the retreat that he thought pain in sitting came from unresolved issues, holding emotion and thoughts in one's body. Is that true? Or, do some people have physical and structural issues in their body or injuries that make sitting difficult. I suspect both are true.

After a few days of sitting, I figured out the "best" combination of pillows, when and how long to sit on the cushion and on the chair, and got into more of a rhythm. After I did that, I didn't feel like I was taking up as much space. I carefully put my pillows in a stack during the walking meditation. If I was using a chair, I pushed it slightly into the center of the room so it wouldn't be in the way as we walked. I tried to be conscious of my needs as well as others.

When traveling, the other people on the bus are not always so conscious of how much space they are using. Some people bring lots of bags (and even chickens) and take up a lot of room in both the overhead spaces and on the floor around their seats. Or perhaps they are conscious of how much space they are using up, but do it anyway out of economic necessity or for some other reason.

On an airplane sitting so close to the people in the same row, I sometimes make up stories about their lives. Other times I choose to be silent and not engage in conversation. Just like at a Zen retreat, we are sitting close to one another but not talking. I imagine how the person is feeling when I see my seatmate holding onto the armrest during take-off. I hear her sigh as she reads her book. I try to see what she is reading. What is the line between being curious and being nosey?

At the Zen retreat, when am I moving from being on my own retreat and projecting about someone else's experience? Is creating a story about someone else's sitting experience or life just a way to divert focus from my own? How do I focus on being present for what is true right now?

Packing Dreams

The packing dreams started not long after my first research trip with Backroads. While the dreams vary, they have a few common characteristics: they seem real, I either never finish packing or I have so many bags that it is next to impossible to get to my next destination. Sometimes the packing is getting ready for a vacation and sometimes the packing involves a move.

Here is one:

I am in a house that has some resemblance to a place that I have lived in the past, or often pieces of different places where I have lived including childhood homes. I am trying to pack up the house in order to move. There is so much stuff and I can't seem to make headway in finishing. Much of the stuff and furniture is packed and gone but there always seems to be more. I thought that there wasn't much left to do and I could get it done in the time I had left, but now am running out of time. I don't have enough boxes, and I can't seem to make progress. It seems so inefficient. Where are other people to help me? The dream ends with no resolution. I feel uneasy when I awake.

The dreams about packing for a trip are similar. I have way too much stuff and can't decide what to take. Sometimes I am already on the trip and I am trying to pack up to move on in my journey. I have so many bags and I can't find them all. Or they are too full. I can't fit everything into the bags that I have. Or some of the bags seem to be missing when I get to the bus stop or train station. Again, these are not pleasant dreams.

These dreams bring up lots of questions. What am I packing for? Am I having a hard time moving on? What do I need to get rid of? Or perhaps I am not ready to move to the next phase of my life? Am I stuck? Am I carrying around too much baggage? How am I burdened? What is holding me back? What do I need to let go of? Do I need to ask for help? Am I missing some pieces?

I packed a small bag for the Zen retreat – my safety net. I didn't really need to pack a bag as I was not spending the night. However, I wanted to be prepared. So, I packed extra socks and my shawl, which I did wear every day. I also packed items that I did not need. I found that my needs on the retreat were actually quite simple. I just needed to show up. I brought some physical and mental baggage with me, but after a few days, some of that baggage seemed to dissipate. The more mundane thoughts started to drop away. The analytical mind relaxed. This quietness allowed for more creative ideas to open up.

Packing in Nepal

Each morning on our trek in Nepal, one of our guides came to our tent to wake us up with a cup of hot *chai* (tea with milk and spices). The warmth and sweet aroma aroused our sleepy bodies. Soon after, he would bring a small tin pan with warm water for washing our face and hands. He brought us a pan of water at night too so that we could take a sponge bath. What a luxury that was. I relished those pans of warm water.

After breakfast, we packed up for the day. Packing was easy. We had our day packs that we carried on our backs. Then we each had a duffle bag which contained our limited set of clothes, a sleeping bag, and pad which were carried by a porter. Actually, the porters each carried two duffle bags tied to their backs, and several of the porters walked barefoot! Or, they would carry the tents. Another porter carried the cooking supplies, including cans of kerosene for cooking. I couldn't imagine being a porter carrying these heavy and stinky loads.

We had it easy. We were well taken care of. Our meals were cooked for us, the path was determined by the guide, and the views of the Himalayas were spectacular. We were given the freedom to appreciate the beauty and starkness around us, to observe our thoughts, and to refrain from complaining about our aches and pains.

Porters carrying our food and fuel

Weather

During the retreat, as we sat in meditation, chanting or eating in the dharma room, we could only hear the rain, not see it. The windows are coated which lets light shine in, but does not allow us to look out or others to see in.

At first during the retreat, I was disappointed that it was raining so much. I was looking forward to taking walks during the breaks and weeding in the garden during work periods. I did still take walks during breaks, but perhaps not as freely. My raincoat hood shielded my head and sometimes I carried an umbrella. With this gear, my body movements felt constrained. I did not walk as far or as fast as I might have had it not been raining.

I liked listening to the rain when I sat in meditation. Sometimes I would hear the rain and sometimes I wouldn't. The rain was still there, it was just a matter of whether I was paying attention to it.

Zen Master Bon Soeng often asks us to pay attention to our likes and dislikes and to not hold them too tightly. One day what I like may become a dislike another day, it is just a matter of perception. I may not like the rain while a gardener may appreciate it. The rain is the same; only our ideas about the rain are different.

Walking Meditation

The *Dharma Mirror* states that "Walking meditation is used as a physical relief period between sitting meditations. During this time people can go out to the bathroom, leave for other reasons, or re-enter the Dharma Room. Since this is still considered meditation, it should not be used as a break..."

The form is to clasp one's hands at the waist with the fingers interweaved and to follow the leader at the pace s/he sets. Sometimes we walk in a big circle around the exterior of the room, sometimes we make a snaking pattern, and if the weather is nice, we may walk on the sidewalk outside the Zen Center. Sometimes we walk slowly and sometimes more quickly. This is determined by the head dharma teacher or whoever is leading the walking meditation.

I found that the walking meditation was a relief, up to a point. What I really wanted to do was to walk more freely with my arms swaying at my side. My body yearned to be stretched and moved in ways that felt good to my body. Walking in a controlled fashion and at someone else's pace did not offer me the relief that I wanted. So, I had the opportunity to examine my desires. In each walking period I decided what I needed. Sometimes I immediately headed out of the room, used the bathroom and then stretched my body in the lounge area. I did some yoga poses to relieve the pain in my body. Sometimes I laid down on my back in *savasana* (corpse pose in yoga) and tried to melt the tension from my back and neck.

Sometimes I began by doing the walking meditation and let my arms swing a bit instead of holding them clasped at my waist. Then I left part way through the walking meditation to stretch. And sometimes I stayed for the entire 10-minute meditation walking in the prescribed manner.

Once Mark and I rented a documentary about Korean nuns on a 90-day meditation retreat (*Zen Buddhism: In Search of Self*). This film does not have much action, as you might guess. I noticed that the way the nuns did walking meditation was different from our form. They moved their arms and walked more freely. My thinking mind believes that their way is better. Our bodies need relief from the controlled way we sit. At least I feel like my body needs to move more freely. What to do with this belief? I decided to allow myself to move a bit more without trying to distract others' practice.

Sometimes during walking meditation I watched how other people walked. I noticed that many people are slightly hunched over in their shoulders. Some are not even, one shoulder leaning down or not squared to the front. I wondered if I too, am uneven in my walk. I think that it would be interesting if someone videotaped our walking meditation so that we could each see how we walk. Then we could offer some body work options to help people correct their alignment, if they chose. I imagine that if we did this, it would help us in our sitting practice too. Thinking, thinking, thinking.

Then I am reminded to pay attention to my walking. Notice the soles of my feet on the floor. Notice my breathing. Notice the sounds in the room. Notice my own body. Pay attention in this moment and just walk.

The Mirror in Nepal and at Home

On our trek in Nepal, I did not have an actual mirror in which to look at myself. And yet I did look at myself and ask a lot of questions. I had the time to do so as I walked long distances each day.

When we travel in remote areas, we may not have a glass mirror. How do we perceive ourselves without a mirror to reflect back? Is it in how others react to us? Or is it in our perceptions of how they react? Is it in reflecting on how they live their lives, their customs, eating practices, family traditions?

One day we came to a *mani* wall, a stone structure with the words *Om mani padme hum*, carved into the rocks in Tibetan. This wall gives travelers the opportunity to pause in their journey. The idea is to walk around the *mani* wall in a clockwise direction and repeat the mantra. The mantra is loosely translated as "behold, the jewel in the lotus."

When I looked in the "mirror" at the Zen Retreat, what did I see? I saw the mirror in the forms – in the chanting, in the formal eating style especially, and in sitting and walking meditation. When

I got annoyed by having to eat so fast, I paused and noticed. I asked myself when else do I get annoyed in my life? Do I want to be in an annoyed state?

In my daily life, I try to incorporate a pause several times during each day. Like walking around the *mani* wall, I get up from my desk and walk around the house, pet my cat, sit quietly on my meditation cushion, go out to the garden and pick a few weeds, or stretch my body. While not repeating the mantra, *om mani padme hum*, I am giving myself the opportunity to step back from work and thought in order to hold up the mirror. Who am I now, in this moment? What or who do I behold?

Mani wall

Awakening Joy

I must admit that one of my favorite parts of the 8-day Zen retreat was the break in the afternoon. Almost every day, despite the rain, I would go for a walk. Sometimes I would walk for the entire period of almost an hour. Other days I would walk to a café and sip coffee and sometimes indulge in a cookie or scone. On the second day of the retreat, I walked quickly up to College Avenue. I noticed that there was no line at *Ici*, a specialty ice cream shop that offers exotic flavors. I ordered a burnt caramel ice cream cone. Oh so yummy. They put a surprise of dark chocolate at the bottom of the crisp homemade cone. I relished every bit of that ice cream cone.

I had to jog the last block back to the Zen Center in order to get back in time. As I sat back down in the Dharma room, I wondered if my ice cream treat was "cheating?" I decided that since I was taking a class entitled, *Awakening Joy*, that this was my bit of joy for the day. This class was teaching me to incline my mind to contentment.

(*Awakening Joy* is a multi-month internet course that is taped in Berkeley, CA and can also be attended in person, which is what I did. James Baraz has taught the course since 2003. He is co-author of a book based on the class entitled, *Awakening Joy*. Each month is devoted to a theme, such as Intention, Gratitude, Mindfulness, Working with Difficult Times and he brings in guest speakers to talk on these themes. I highly recommend the class.)

Where is the joy in an hour of chanting?

When I first started practicing at the Empty Gate Zen Center, the part of practice that I found most challenging was chanting. What is the purpose of chanting? What do the words mean? Even the chants in English seem like *gobbeldy gook*. Some people seem to really enjoy it, how is that? Some have beautiful singing voices and use them to sing out the chants. I can't do that. I wish we would chant in a different key. I try to sing it high, then I move an octave lower and just can't seem to find a comfortable range in my voice to sing. My mind wanders and then I get lost and can't find my place in the chant book.

Why can't it be more like *kirtan* (Indian devotional music) with Krishna Das? I like that. His voice is so beautiful and I like the way the chanting is done in a call and response fashion. Plus he sings in a key that works for my voice. I tell myself, "Well Sue, this is not *kirtan*. It is different. So, get over your likes and dislikes already."

Over the course of attending the Zen Center more regularly, especially on Wednesday nights, the chanting has gotten easier for me. Or maybe I should say that I have accepted it as part of the practice and don't fight it. The singing key is still not good for my limited vocal range. Now I just do it and don't evaluate or resist it like I did when I started. I have accepted that this is the form of chanting done in the Kwan Um School of Zen and I try to just be with it whether I like it or not.

Chanting, like the other forms of practice, is one of the ways we can watch our minds. How do my likes and dislikes get in the way of my just being? What can I learn about myself as I watch my struggle with chanting? How is my reaction to chanting similar or different from other activities that I am uncomfortable with in my life?

I became accustomed to chanting on Wednesday nights for a half hour. But chanting on a retreat was an entirely different story. The evening chant period is an hour. One chant has us bowing and chanting at the same time. My reaction the first couple of nights went something like, "What is up with this? How am I supposed to hold and read the chant book if I am down on my knees with my head bent? How do I make this work if I want to sit in a chair and not on the cushion?"

The *Thousand Hands and Eyes Sutra* that we chant in Korean is seven and a half pages and goes so fast, includes an unbearable number of syllables and seems to be endless. "This is impossible and frustrating. There is no way I can get my tongue around these syllables."

First phrase of six on page one of the *Thousand Hands and Eyes Sutra* chant:

> a-gum il-shim-jung
> juk-kyun mu-jin-shin
> byon-je gwan-um dae-song-jon
> il-il mu-su-rye
> om ba-a-ra mil
> om ba-a-ra mil
> om ba-a-ra mil

Now try to chant the above quickly. You will get the idea of my challenge in wrapping my head, tongue and voice around six pages of this chant at night when I was tired and ready to be home already.

"Do these syllables mean anything? Why should I be chanting something I don't even understand? Maybe I am repeating stuff I wouldn't want to be saying if I knew what it meant. I'm tired and I don't want to be doing this. This is ridiculous."

Boy, did I sound like a whiner. Clearly, I still had things to learn from the experience and process of chanting. Little did I know that my experience with chanting was not too different from others. A couple of years later, I read the following excerpt from the forward to the Kwan Um School of Zen chant book by Zen Master Seung Sahn.

> In our Zen Centers, people live together and practice together. At first, people come with strong opinions, strong likes and dislikes. (He got that right!) For many people, chanting meditation is not so easy: much confused thinking, many likes and dislikes. (Bingo!) But when we do chanting meditation correctly, perceive the sound of our own voice and the voices all around us, our minds become clear. In clear mind, there is no like or dislike, only the sound of the voice.

The practice of chanting is guiding me to practice: "In clear mind, there is no like or dislike, only the sound of the voice."

Pain in Nepal

I experienced a lot of pain in Nepal just as I did sitting still on a meditation cushion. As in the Zen retreat, the pain was both physical and mental. As we hiked past children along our path, I felt sad seeing that they were barefoot and dirty and had snot coming out of their noses. They were very poor and I imagined that they had little or no access to medical care or education. They begged for candy. I certainly didn't want to contribute to their tooth decay, yet I also felt a sense of yearning to do something for them. Sometimes we gave the children pencils and small note pads, a cheap toy, or let them look through our cameras. I felt like these small gestures were not enough. As in a Zen retreat, we may see someone that we think is in pain and there may not be anything we can do, at least at the time.

I also had physical pain as I hiked up and down the mountain trails. My knees especially ached hiking downhill. Prior to one particularly steep climbing day, our Sherpa guide found long sturdy sticks and fashioned walking poles for us. They were welcome tools. He demonstrated how to use the poles to reduce our effort.

On the day that we were at our highest elevation so far, at the base of Langtang at 11,000 feet, I had a blazing headache. It was so bad that I felt nauseous. I hardly slept that night. The next day we awoke before dawn to hike up a nearby peak from where we would be treated to spectacular views. The climb was very steep and over large boulders. I walked slower than I ever thought was possible. One step at a time. Step. Breathe. Step. Breathe. Our group ended up divided between two who were faster and way ahead, and the rest of us.

One of our group members was having a particularly tough time. He ended up getting disoriented and had "sewing machine leg." That is a descriptive term for loss of control of the muscles; his leg was bouncing up and down uncontrollably. A guide and a porter got along side of him and started to walk him back down the mountain to our camp. He was better once he was at a lower elevation.

Soon the fog came in. For those of us slower, we had missed our opportunity to see the views from the top. We too decided to turn around and head back to camp. While I was looking forward to seeing the views and feeling the satisfaction of making it to the top, the decision to turn around and head back was made easily due to the heavy fog.

Two members of our group plus our Sherpa guide reached the peak in time to capture what they later told us was a spectacular view of the surrounding and distant mountains. We spent the rest of the day in camp on one of our few layover days. A cold stream passed through the camp so we took sponge baths and washed our socks. My head continued to hurt but not quite as bad as the first night at that elevation.

I learned that despite the pain, in my head and in my knees, I could keep going. If I took it slow and rested, I would be able to progress onward. What other choice did I have? I was in the middle of the mountains with no roads. It would have required extreme measures to get myself out of that situation. I persevered and worked through the pain.

Could I do the same on the Zen retreat?

Author and Bim proudly pose at the top of a mountain pass.

The Third Day

And on the third day I finally had a bowel movement. Not unlike going on vacation when my routine is often uprooted, the retreat also changed my sleeping, eating and coffee drinking schedule. And this led to a disruption of my digestive system. Once I had a bowel movement, I believe this led to less pain in my back. Or maybe I am making this up. Just another story I am telling myself? It is often difficult to know what follows from what.

I had lined myself up to give the dharma talk on the Wednesday night after the end of the retreat. Wednesday nights at the Empty Gate Zen Center are a bit different than other nights. The evening begins at 7 p.m. with a half hour of chanting, then a bit of instruction on our sitting style, then 25 minutes of sitting. This is followed by a dharma talk of 10 -20 minutes by a person who has taken at least five precepts. Then our Zen Master comments or adds to the talk and opens up the evening to questions and comments from anyone. The evening ends by 9 p.m. This is often the night when newcomers are introduced to the Zen Center but also a time that everyone enjoys because it is more social and includes some "instruction" on Zen.

I had purposely signed up to give the first dharma talk after the retreat because I was pretty sure that I would have something to say, and it would be fresh in my mind. I could talk about what it was like for me to sit an 8-day retreat. So on day three, I started composing in my head the beginning of my dharma talk. I found myself crafting a talk around what I was feeling, thinking, experiencing. I asked myself, "Should I share this? What about this thought? What will people want to hear?"

These thoughts then flowed into an internal discussion about religious choice. I wondered whether certain religious or spiritual traditions, especially those that people choose as adults, attract certain personality types. For example, does Zen attract people who like structure and perhaps are a bit anal? Maybe people who are attracted to *Vipassana* meditation are not as rigid? Then I thought that this could be the topic of a doctoral dissertation. Then I thought, wait, I could do the research and write a book. Then I thought, who cares what personality types are attracted to which religion, if this is even so? How does answering this question advance our knowledge or contribute to the greater good?

My mind was active. I was enjoying playing with these ideas. I also began playing with the idea of a Zen retreat being like a vacation. When a friend said to me in the week prior to the retreat, "have fun," I thought to myself, "yeah, right." But as I sat, I thought about all of the other aspects of a vacation, in addition to fun, that are or can be similar to a retreat.

Over the next few days, during breaks from sitting, I jotted down a long list of similarities including:

Preparation – planning, anticipation, reading about what to expect and what to do, packing, choosing accommodations.

THE THIRD DAY

On the vacation – fellow travelers, sleep, change of diet and digestion issues, modes of travel, meeting new people, new ways of perceiving and doing things, feelings of belonging and separateness, rituals, bargaining, getting lost, finding a new path, trip leaders, beauty, and the list goes on...

Reflections – how are we alike and different, would I want to live there, new friends, stories about my vacation, there's no place like home...

And as I sat, more ideas came to me. It reminded me of when I was a college student and in one of my classes we were asked to keep a journal. This was the first time that I had written in a journal on a regular basis. Once I got into it, I constantly "wrote" my journal in my head. I had a job in food service that started at 6 am. I walked to work in the dark and "wrote" in my journal as I walked. The journal was always with me whether I was actually physically writing in it or not. I constantly paid attention to what was around and in my thoughts and considered whether to write about it later.

At the retreat, I was thinking, thinking, thinking. My mind was not at all still. I allowed myself to go where all this thinking took me. Then gradually, the thoughts started to slow down. It was as if I had exhausted all of my thoughts.

By the third day, I had a better idea of why I was sitting the retreat and even imagined, amazingly, that perhaps I would do this again someday. Also by the third day, I started to understand in a new way some of the Zen teachings that I had listened to for many years.

One night, prior to the last sitting period, the bell rang indicating it was time to go back into the dharma room. I thought to myself, "Another round of hell." I laughed and then decided to turn my thinking around. Rather than "make" something of it, I just said to myself, "Last sitting period."

Another time I caught myself making up a story about others in the dharma room. I was aware that someone was fidgeting or perhaps crying or maybe I noticed that someone was missing from his or her cushion. I would start to make up a story about what I imagined was going on for them. Then I thought, we never really know what the experience is of someone else. We can only ask the person or wait for them to tell us. Someone I think may be crying tears of pain, may instead be crying tears of joy. Or maybe they aren't crying at all.

When we travel, especially when we don't understand the language, we may fall into the trap of misinterpretation. We may visit a temple and watch a ritual and make an assumption about what is going on. I remember in Bali seeing men holding hands on the streets. I didn't know how to interpret that. Were they gay or is it more common for men to have physical contact in public in Bali?

When it came time to give my dharma talk, I decided to only mention in passing the analogy between a vacation and retreat. I talked about it in terms of preparing to go on vacation and the similarities of preparing to go on retreat. I decided that I wanted to develop this idea further, perhaps in the form of a book, and wasn't ready to make the ideas public. There were plenty of other retreat experiences to share in my dharma talk.

Original Face
Poem by Zen Master Seung Sahn

Your true self is always
shining and free.
Human beings make something
and enter the ocean of suffering.

Only without thinking
can you return to your true self.
The high mountain is always blue.
White clouds coming, going.

Chitwan Jungle in Nepal

After our 10-day trek in the Himalayas and a few days exploring in Kathmandu, Lisa and I flew to Pokhara where we walked around town and visited with friends of Lisa's. We booked a 3-night stay at the Chitwan Jungle Lodge in an inner terai valley in the Southern grassland area of Nepal near the border of India. A young man arrived at our lodging to transport us to the Chitwan Jungle Lodge. Soon he stopped at another guest house and picked up the married couple, "Cheryl" and "Craig". We were quite surprised to learn that they too were from the San Francisco Bay Area. A small world indeed.

The ride to Chitwan jungle was hot and long, and for me, made even longer by Cheryl's constant chatter. After we learned about each other's work and where we had traveled, Cheryl started a running commentary on what she was seeing out the window. It was as if the dialogue that she would be having in her head was instead being spoken out loud for us all to hear. "Look at that sign. I wonder what that means? My, that boy is dirty. Coca-Cola. I am so hot. Why aren't they wearing shoes?" And on and on and on. I allowed myself to get very annoyed by her incessant observations and commentary.

I now realize that had this been twenty years later, I might have reacted differently to her. Perhaps I would have asked myself what about her behavior was so annoying to me. What lesson could I glean from this experience? At the time, I did none of this self-reflection. I only felt like she was tormenting me and it wasn't fair because I was on vacation.

About an hour from our destination she wasn't feeling well. All of a sudden she stopped talking as she appeared to have some kind of stomach problem. When we got to the Chitwan jungle, a young man escorted us to our cabins and told us lunch would be served shortly. At the dining hall, a Nepali waiter showed us to our table. Soon, Craig was also ushered in and sat at our table. "I am so sorry that Cheryl can't be here," he apologized. "She is not feeling well." I gulped selfishly and thought, "Oh no. They are not going to make us sit with this couple for every meal of our stay here, are they?" Craig excused himself from lunch early so he could tend to Cheryl.

I looked at Lisa and said, "We have got to do something about this." She looked at me like, what can we do? I told her, "Now is the time when your Nepali language skills can really come in handy. You must talk to the wait staff and ask them if we can sit with different people in the future." She mustered up the courage and began a conversation with two of the waiters. They seemed perplexed. She wasn't sure if she had communicated our desires correctly.

At dinner that night we were ushered to the same table we had sat at lunch. Lisa and I looked at each other with disappointment. In a few minutes Craig came in and the waiter took him to a table across the way. He looked at us and raised his hands and shoulders in an "I don't know" expression. We did the same. Then they brought a lovely German couple to our table. Lisa and I smiled at each other with relief and just a bit of guilt.

The next day we went out on a jungle walk just outside the lodging compound with two armed naturalists. They warned in a whisper, "Be very quiet and stay together." They pointed out birds, an ant hill and various trees. Again they said, "Stay close together. It is dangerous out here." My cynical-self thought that this is all part of the adventure and hype. They are making a rather mundane walk seem like more than it is.

Then, suddenly, I saw a flash of movement in the tree just six feet ahead. My body tensed. I glimpsed the rear of a tiger jump down from the tree and another flash of movement as what appeared to be a second tiger also made a giant leap and ran away. It all happened so fast I wasn't sure what I had really seen.

Our guides were shocked. They quickly brought us all together and clearly they were surprised by what they had just seen. "I guess we aren't in Disneyland," I thought. We headed back to camp. Then our guides could talk more freely, "We have never seen a tiger before on a jungle walk. That could have been very dangerous."

Lisa and I looked at each other both thinking, "That was awesome" and then we gradually felt fear.

The guides reminded us, "Do not walk outside of the camp grounds and always be accompanied by a guide when it is dark, even to go to your cabin." Now the rules that they told us when we first arrived at the lodge made a lot more sense to us.

Sometimes things are not what they seem. As Zen Master Bon Soeng would often say, "Be careful. Watch your step." At the end of the temple rules is a poem written by the founder of the Kwan Um School of Zen, Zen Master Soeng Sahn:

> In the great work of life and death,
>   time will not wait for you.
> If you die tomorrow, what kind of body will you get?
> Is not all of this of great importance?
> Hurry up! Hurry!
> Blue sky and green sea are the Buddha's original
>   face.
> The sound of the waterfall and the bird's song
>   are the great sutras.
> Where are you going?
> Watch your step.
> Water flows down to the sea.
> Clouds float up to the heavens.

What kind of karma did I make for myself in the way I treated Cheryl? The tiger leaping from the tree woke me up that day in the Chitwan jungle.

Sleep Or Lack There Of

During the retreat I was not getting my normal eight hours of sleep. Even though I wasn't "doing" much, I felt fuzzy during the first few days. Then after a few days, even though I wasn't getting additional sleep, my mind began to feel clearer and I felt more awake. It could have been due to getting into the rhythm of the retreat. I also allowed myself to take little catnaps during a couple of the sitting periods rather than fight it. My mind relaxed, my body relaxed, and I felt a bit less pain as I sat. I was thinking less about mundane things. I stopped much of the planning, calculating, rehearsing, theorizing about Zen retreats. I stopped thinking about my work. I then began to have more creative thoughts.

I imagined that the reason there are so many books on Zen is that people who sit come up with the ideas for their books while in meditation. Throughout the retreat I thought of more and more ideas of how a Zen retreat is like traveling. During breaks in sitting, I made notes in my journal. I now had a focus for my retreat and I felt energized.

I also imagined that in another retreat, I might have a very different experience. If I were going through something challenging in my life at the time, the lack of sleep could contribute to heightened emotions. However, this was not the case for me at this retreat.

From retreat days 3 to 5, I spent a portion of each day thinking about the commonalities of a retreat and a vacation. It felt creative and fun. But I didn't spend all my time thinking about this. I also had some periods of clarity or pointedness where I was simply paying attention to breathing in and out. And with less thinking, the sitting periods seemed to be longer.

Seeing

As I sat on my cushion with my eyes slightly open (which is the Kwan Um School of Zen style), I noticed a spot on the floor that I had not seen before. How could that be? I had been sitting for four days. Throughout that day I remembered to look at that spot on the floor, really see it, and I realized that it changed as the natural light changed. During a break, I went over to look at the spot on the floor up close and realized it was just a slight imperfection in the wood. At night, with the overhead lights on, it wasn't visible at all.

It reminded me of when I was in my early 20's and my boyfriend studied plant ecology. We went hiking and eventually stopped and sat down in a field. John suggested that we look at the small area just in front of us and see how many different plants we could spot. At first, it didn't seem like that many. But then, as we continued to sit, got comfortable and let our vision both open up and focus in, we were amazed at how many different plants that we spotted in a very small area.

So often we don't see what is right in front of us. Here I was in the dharma room with very few distractions from daily life, yet I hadn't noticed what was right in front of me. Not only do we ignore what is physically right in front of us, but we often filter our thoughts. We listen to some thoughts but not others.

In 1982, I had moved back to California from Minnesota and was looking for a job. I was living with my brother temporarily in Mill Valley and had applied for a position at San Jose State University. It was a position that was a step or two backwards in my career and not something that I particularly wanted to do. However, the job market was tight so I applied anyway. I interviewed and was offered the position.

Now what do I do? I got in my car and headed south to San Jose and explored various neighborhoods to see where I might live. I remember somehow always ending up on Camino Real, a street that at the time had a lot of car dealerships, fast food restaurants, and other types of businesses that were not attractive to me. I was having a difficult time picturing myself living in this area.

As I drove back to my temporary home, I thought about the job and whether I should take it. Tears streamed down my face unexpectedly. At first I wondered why and tried to dismiss them. Then, I realized that I needed to pay attention to what my body was telling me. "Sue, don't take this job. You can find a better match." I slept on that decision and the next day I called to tell them that I decided not to take the position. They were surprised, but I never regretted the decision.

I paid attention to what was right in front of me. My emotions and body told me that this was not the right job for me. I needed to wait to find something that was a better fit. Had I ignored what was right in front of me, in fact rolling down my face, I may have taken the job. And, who knows what would have happened then? I may not have ended up working later at Backroads, which gave me so many opportunities to not only travel but to learn so much.

One of my old travel journals included the quote written by the English writer, G. K. Chesterton (1874–1936): "The traveler sees what he sees; the tripper sees what he has come to see."

Zen teachers offer that seeing and hearing are already the truth. The sky is blue. The floor is brown. As a traveler in Bali I may see a woman place on the ground a leaf arranged with flowers and rice atop it. I see this and notice it but I may not know why she puts it there or what it means. Through asking questions and reading about the ritual, I may gain some understanding about it. However I am an observer of her practice. She may be experiencing this ritual as a devotional act, or as a routine that she just does each morning, or perhaps it is a special day that day. I can't really know that for sure.

Zen Master Bon Soeng would remind us of this point during his Dharma talks. If someone honks their car horn at me for some unknown reason, it doesn't necessarily mean they are being an asshole. I don't know what is going on in that person's life at that moment. If I can maintain my composure, I can keep the incident from escalating and my blood pressure from rising. I simply hear a car horn blow. Perhaps I will also observe something about my own driving.

If I see what is in front of me, then I will likely see more than if I see what I have come to see. If I plan a vacation at the beach and it rains for several days, I will surely be disappointed. However, if I complain and am in a bad mood the entire time, I will miss out on what other possibilities may arise if I keep my eyes open. I might meet an interesting person in the café who is also there seeking shelter from the rain.

Trusting in Thailand

Suzy was one of the bike trip leaders of the first Backroads trips to Bali on which I was a "guest." Suzy is like the energizer bunny and always up for an adventure, so she and I headed to Thailand for further adventures at the conclusion of the Bali trip. After several days exploring Bangkok, walking the crowded sidewalks with big eyes feasting on the sights and sounds, sampling the spicy Thai dishes, and visiting temples and museums, we booked a second class sleeper train to Chiang Mai in the northern part of the country.

The overnight train trip was clean, efficient and safe. I slept surprisingly well. As we walked from the train station to the guest house we had chosen from our tour book, we saw several posters describing hill tribe treks. We hadn't planned to do one, but suddenly the power of advertising was enticing us to consider a trek.

We soon arrived at SK House, with a lovely front room from which they sold hill tribe crafts. They told us about a 2 night/3 day trek that would be departing in a half hour. Did we want to go? We could leave some of our belongings at the guest house and they would even buy our return train ticket to Bangkok for us so that we would have it when we got back. And, they would make sure we had a room at the inn for the night we returned from the trek. It all sounded good.

We handed over 1800 baht each for the train ticket and 1000 baht for the trek. (At 25 baht to the dollar, that was $72 for the train trip and $40 for the trek.) It dawned on us once we were on the trek that we were very trusting. Would they really buy our train ticket for us? Would our packs still be there when we returned?

Within no time a truck pulled up. We were the last two of eight trekkers plus our Thai guide and his "sister." Later we all decided that she was most likely the guide's girlfriend. The other trekkers were Europeans plus one solo male Japanese medical student. The two-hour trip in the back of the truck was hot and uncomfortable. We sat on narrow parallel benches. The sides and top of the truck were covered with a thick canvas. We bounced along and could not see any of the passing scenery, only our fellow travelers who were not that pretty to look at.

We were relieved when we were told we would walk the final two hours to the first village, as the dirt road was too rutted and washed out to carry us. The air was thick with smoke. It was hot, dry and ugly. Supposedly, at other times of the year, we would have seen views of the green, terraced hills. By now I was already wondering what we were doing there.

We trudged past burning fields and hillsides. We weren't sure what was going on but wondered if they were burning the fields after harvesting their crops, possibly including poppies. We finally arrived at the Meo tribe village, where we stayed that night. The children's thin bodies and clothes were covered in dirt and their eyes were glassy and sad. They begged for candy and baht.

The children didn't smile or laugh and their parents yelled at them. The women sat outside their shacks embroidering fabric. There was one tiny store that sold water, candy and odds and ends. The only water source for the village appeared to be a pipe with a thin stream of water. The homes were made of bamboo and cooking was done in a fire pit inside the house on the dirt floor. There were a total of three trekking groups staying in this small village, and we each slept in a different home, displacing the family that would normally sleep there.

Suzy and hill tribe children

I feared that the treks brought more harm than good to the village. Trekkers would buy candy for the kids. Any money that was paid to the families was most likely used to buy opium, at least that is what appeared to be going on. Much of the time we were in the village, I kept asking myself, "what is going on here?"

After a dinner of rice, vegetables, and I think chicken, our guide told us a bit about the tribe and the opium trade. He said that the opium poppies were taken to Burma where they were made into heroin. He told us that the owner of the home where we stayed was an opium addict. Later, another man in the village took our group to see a rummy game being played for money and we saw our guide lose big. Then he took us to see a man lying on his side smoking opium, seemingly oblivious to our presence. Our new guide asked us if we wanted to try opium. No one in our group took him up on it, but we did see other trekkers doing so. Then he took us to see a woman whom he said was 125 years old. Her daughter was trying to feed her a thin broth. I felt very uncomfortable on this tour of the village. While I was fascinated to see people and things that I had never witnessed before, I felt like he was putting these people on display for us. What must the villagers have thought of us? What are we doing here?

We slept, or at least attempted to, on the bamboo mats on the dirt floor in the one room of the house. We were each given two blankets. Fortunately I had brought a sleep sheet along because those blankets didn't look too clean. I did not sleep well that night.

As we started walking the next morning, just on the edge of the village, we saw the young man who had been hired to carry our food lying on the floor in a shack smoking opium. We wondered if we would see him and our food later that day. It was a long, hot hike on sometimes narrow and steep trails. We crossed several streams on rocks and logs – not one of my favorite things to do. We arrived at our lunch destination, a Karen tribe outpost. We cooled our feet in the stream. Some in our group sat in the water. Later, we saw elephants being bathed in the stream. I began to pray that we would not pick up a parasite on this hill tribe trek.

Finally our lunch porter arrived. He set down the basket of food and then he laid his body down and began smoking a seemingly endless round of pipes of opium. People in our group took photos of him and the medical student lifted the porter's wrist and monitored his pulse. Again, I was seriously questioning what we were doing here and the negative effects of these treks on the hill tribes.

Our lunch soup was prepared from water dug from a hole next to the river. Amazingly, we all ate the soup and none of us appeared to get sick. That afternoon was the elephant-ride segment of the trek. Suzy and I had not paid for this part of the tour package, but we had to wait along with everyone else for the elephants to arrive. And wait and wait and wait.

When the elephants finally did come, from where we were not sure, they had to be bathed in the river that we had sat in earlier to cool off. They were then covered with mats and then a wood frame was placed on their backs. Three people sat on each elephant, two in the frame and the elephant guide straddling the elephant's neck using his feet to give directions. The elephants moved incredibly slowly. Occasionally they would blow snot all over their guides and passengers. We waited for all of the elephants to get on their way and then quickly caught up with them as we walked with our guide and "his sister" crossing streams over rocks and then eventually just walking in the water.

In the next village, of the Karen tribe, the homes were larger, cleaner and made of teak-wood built on stilts. Lots of cows and pigs ran around. These villagers appeared to be better off, probably because of their proximity to the river.

Dinner was served out on the "deck" of our home for the night. We toasted my companion, Suzy, as it was her birthday. At one point, Suzy climbed down the ladder to find a place to "pee" and proceeded to fall into the mud where the pigs bathed. Just before that she had shown off her Velcro sandals (a new innovation in sandals at that time) which were now covered in mud.

Karen tribe house

That night we slept on the hard teak surface and it was cold. I had had a headache all day and it did not go away that night. The next morning we arose early for the next phase of this trek – a "raft" trip down the river. Our rafts consisted of nine long bamboo poles with five shorter cross poles that were tied together with bamboo strips. In the upper third portion three sticks were tied together in a vertical triangle. From this structure they hung our packs. Much to our surprise, we were told that we would be standing on this raft for the four hour trip down the river in the hot sun.

We had to focus on keeping our balance as there was nothing to hold onto. This was not what we expected when they advertised rafting on this trek.

The river was low with many exposed rocks. A few in our group fell off of the raft but fortunately, no one landed on a rock. I fell to my knees once and scraped them up. Thankfully, I did not get an infection from the cuts. The raft trip was actually fun at first and exciting as we navigated the small rapids. But after two hours, I had had enough. Occasionally I would sit down on the raft in the six inches of water that floated over the top. At one point, our raft leader spotted a small snake in the water. He attempted to kill it, but it got loose. He then instructed us to be careful. "Be careful?! How are we supposed to do that?" I have no idea whether the snake was poisonous. From then on, most of us decided not to sit on the raft anymore, even though we were hot and tired of standing and balancing for so long.

Rafting in Thailand

This trek in the hill country of Thailand, as it turned out, offered other potential dangers. We were only three walking days from the Thai/Burma border where there was periodic fighting as well as drug raids. I suppose ignorance is bliss, especially when nothing bad happened to us.

The last village we arrived at was quite developed. Their homes had "patios" and cross-thatched roofs and sides. There were also quite a few westerners there. As we stepped off of the rafts, we were immediately greeted by hill tribe women wanting to sell us their hand-made goods. A truck met six members of our group to take us back to Chiang Mai. The others were staying for another night. I was glad to be heading back. That trek was definitely a learning experience, and it was also uncomfortable on many levels. I am glad I did it, but I would certainly not do it again.

A Zen retreat is also uncomfortable in many respects, yet I would do a retreat again. The difference is that while a Zen retreat may be physically uncomfortable and often mentally as well, it is not dangerous and it does not potentially harm others.

Back at our guesthouse in Chiang Mai we were shown to Room One, next to the outdoor kitchen. Our packs were in our room as were our train tickets. We felt relieved that our trust in them was warranted. However, the room was dirty, but we were so tired and dirty ourselves that we didn't ask for a different one, much to our regret. We showered in the disgusting shower stall, rested on our thin mattresses, and then went out for dinner and to the famous night market. We were overwhelmed by all of the goods in the market – hill tribe weavings and embroidery, silver jewelry, handmade quilts and much more. I bought several decorative pillow covers, silver earrings to give to the female staff at work, a woven jacket for my mom which she wore until it was threadbare. We worked ourselves into a shopping frenzy and neither of us are shopaholics.

That night I couldn't sleep thinking about which gift I was going to give to whom and lusting after more items in the market. I also couldn't sleep because I was itching all over. It turns out that there were tiny bugs in our beds.

The next day, our plan was to rent bicycles and ride to the town where artisans hand painted paper umbrellas. Our innkeeper told us it was too hot for that and suggested instead that she get us a driver who would take us to six factories: silk, wood, lacquer ware, silver, ceramic, and umbrella. We went with her plan. The first stop was the silk factory.

After a brief tour of the factory where we saw how the silk was made, we ended up in the showroom. We were impressed with the rich and brightly colored silk fabrics. I saw an intricate silk quilt made up of small pastel geometric pieces. After much pondering, I decided to buy it. It was a lot of money for me ($160) but they did throw in four silk pillow covers. For many years that beautiful and elegant quilt covered my bed. I still have it, though it is in the closet now after having ripped in a few places.

We happened to see two of our German trek companions at the silk factory. They told us that they were having silk suits made. After spending a long time at the first factory, we left for the wood factory. While there, Suzy got into her head that we should go back to the silk factory and get our own silk suits made. I was a bit reluctant after my quilt purchase, but agreed. We managed to tell our driver what we wanted to do. He looked at us quizzically but seemed to understand as he did drive us back there.

We looked through fashion magazines and pattern books to decide on an outfit that we each wanted sewn. Then we chose fabric. I picked out a sleeveless sheath dress to be made out of a silk fan-patterned material with a jacket made of a solid fuchsia-colored silk. Suzy choose a skirt and jacket made of a deep blue fabric. The staff measured our bodies and took our orders. Since we were heading back to Bangkok that night on the train, we arranged for them to mail our new outfits to California. That also meant that we would not have a fitting. We paid $100 total for the fabric and sewing, plus $30 for shipping. They said that the outfits would arrive in two weeks. Once again we were very trusting.

We then set off with our young driver to the other factories. We were already exhausted and we had four more factories to visit. These we managed to check out more quickly and limited our shopping as we had already more than shot our wad. After a late lunch we went back to the night market for a bit more shopping before heading to the train station with all of our purchases.

We arrived in Bangkok in the morning and took a taxi to the home of a friend of a friend with whom we had stayed prior to going to Chiang Mai. We showered, did a load of laundry and then called for a taxi to meet us at the Imperial Hotel at 1 p.m. Our host suggested a taxi was the best way for us to travel to Aranyapratet, a town near the border with Cambodia. We were going to visit an acquaintance, "Mike," who was an official with the United Nations Border Relief Operation (UNBRO).

We waited in the lobby of the hotel for 20 minutes for the taxi to show up. Finally we asked a woman at the hotel if she would call the taxi number for us. They told her that they would not pick us up at the hotel. We had to take a different taxi to their taxi station a mile away. Who knows how long we could have waited there if we hadn't finally asked someone to help us.

When we arrived at the dark and creepy taxi garage, we were directed to our taxi. We gulped as we saw the beat up car. The driver was an older gentleman who borrowed someone else's glasses to read the piece of paper on which was written our destination in Thai. He examined the piece of paper for a long time before I asked for it back and then took it over to a woman sitting at a desk. I asked her if the man knew where this place was. She assured me that he did. Mind you all of this is being done in English, as we spoke no Thai. We just hoped that they knew enough English to understand us.

We put our belongings in the trunk. My new silk quilt sat on top of our packs. We soon discovered that the car had no air conditioning. With the windows open, the car exhaust filled the inside of the car. Next we noticed that the front seat was tied on with a rope. We slowly made our way through the gridlocked traffic of Bangkok. I heard a banging noise and thought that the car must need new shock absorbers, which it did. Then I realized that the trunk was open. We tapped the driver on the shoulder and motioned to the trunk. He shook his head in understanding but kept driving. I had visions of my new quilt flying out of the trunk. Finally, just before he was to get on the freeway, he swerved to the side of the road, stopped and managed to close the trunk by slamming it down several times. Suzy and I looked at each other and gulped.

About an hour into the four-hour hot, sticky drive, the passenger door in the front flew open for no apparent reason. For the next three hours of the trip, I wondered if we were going where we wanted to be going. Finally, we saw a sign with the name of the town, Aranyapratet. What a relief. I kept thinking about how trusting we were. Who knows where we could have ended up?

We passed many military bases and checkpoints. It was spooky. At one, they checked our driver's papers. The soldiers looked at us and we looked back at them with sweat on our brow and sleepy eyes.

We finally reached the UNBRO office and Mike was not there. He was out at Site 2, one of the border camps. We were driven by a staff person to his comfortable (and hot) house to relax until he came back. We both pulled reports off his bookshelf that described the refuge situation in Thailand. Mike appreciated when people would take the trip out to the border so that they could see firsthand what the camps were like and then bring this information back home with them.

In 1988, when we were there, the Thai government placed rules on what could and could not go on in the camps as they did not want the Cambodians thinking that Thailand would be their new permanent home. The Thai government saw the camps as a temporary respite. The refugees were not allowed to work or sell any items. There was no land for them to farm. Consequently, there was a lot of idleness and they were becoming dispirited. Mike told us that physical abuse was on the rise. The refugees would try to sell some of their rice allotment to the Thais so that they would have money to buy other food items or cigarettes.

There were many relief organizations working in the camps including the Red Cross, Care, a variety of Christian organizations and other NGO's. We were scheduled to visit the camps the next afternoon. Amazingly, the first "incident" to happen in a year near the camps occurred the next morning. Two bandits stopped a water truck on the road to the camps and forced the driver out of his vehicle. They told him to flag down other passing vehicles. One vehicle, he waved to continue on and the bandits shot at the car as it drove by. When the next vehicle came by, the driver was forced to make them stop.

The bandits took a female relief worker as a hostage. Eventually, the Thai police arrived and intervened. One of the bandits was killed, two Thai police officers were wounded and the relief workers were shook up. We didn't know any of this as we waited at Mike's home for him to pick us up later in the day. Mid-morning he called to tell us what was going on.

We had lunch with Mike and a Red Cross official at the UNHRC café. They talked in hushed tones fearful that their conversation might be overheard by someone. I was not clear about who they thought might be listening. I strained to hear and understand what they were saying. What was clear is that we were lucky that Mike had not taken us out to the camps in the morning as that could have been us held up. Mike said that we had to cancel our afternoon visit to the camps.

Even though we were not able to see the camps, I was glad we had made the journey out to this remote part of Thailand. This was certainly not on the tourist circuit and I learned so much more than I ever would have about the situation on the border.

We took the late afternoon bus back to Bangkok. Suzy and I couldn't figure out why they had recommended the taxi on the way there. The bus was only 100 baht and it was comfortable and air conditioned. As we headed back, we talked about our many Thai adventures. We got a taste of the political, economic and social issues that the Thai people, the northern hill tribes and the

Cambodian refugees faced. We returned home with more compassion and a desire to learn more about this region of the world. Now when we read in the newspaper about Thailand or Cambodia, we had a bit more understanding of the area. We were more awake to what was happening each day in this part of the world.

Laughter in the Dharma Room

Mealtime in the dharma room tended to be the time when I experienced the most emotion and judgment as well as frustration, annoyance with the process, both an ability to go with the flow and a desire to resist it, and laughter.

Earlier I described the time when I laughed uncontrollably over a seemingly small incident. Toward the end of the retreat, I also shared a laughing moment with Mark. At the end of each meal, we dry three of our four bowls with our yellow wash rag and then stack the bowls. The fourth bowl contains the leftover water from the bowl cleaning process. The person who finishes drying the three bowls first, rises and gets the ceramic bowl from the mat in the center of the room. Starting with the Zen Master, he stops in front of each person to collect the water from their fourth bowl. They pour this water into the ceramic bowl, being careful not to let any food particles enter the bowl.

On this day, I finished eating first and looked at Zen Master Bon Soeng. He motioned with his eyes for me to get up and get the ceramic bowl. I did so, stopping in front of each person as they poured varying amounts of water into it. Some had bowls with very clean water so they dumped the entire contents into the larger ceramic bowl. Others dumped half of their water. I continued counter clockwise around the room until I reached Mark. Mark dropped one drop of water into the bowl. We both started laughing.

Mark is a messy eater. At home, when we finish a meal, his placemat is often covered with crumbs. His cloth napkin covered with *schmutz*. So, it didn't surprise me that he only poured in one drop, but then again it did take me by surprise. We shared our own private joke.

However, the next person that I needed to go to with the bowl was Robert, the head dharma teacher and the leader of the retreat. His job was to check the ceramic bowl and to indicate whether the water in it was clean or dirty. If the water is clear, he gives the okay sign. If it is dirty he wags his finger. At this retreat the water bowl was almost always given the finger wag. I was still laughing when I got to Robert, but this time I was able to collect myself and the laughter ended quickly. I then took the bowl to the kitchen and emptied it into the sink in three portions as prescribed.

The instructions for formal meals take up 6 pages in the *Dharma Mirror*. Here are some excerpts to give you a flavor for the rules.

> Our four-bowl eating style is a modification of the form used in Korean monasteries.
> Originally, in Buddha's time, there was only one bowl. The four bowls are symbolic of the four elements (earth, air, fire and water) and also of Buddha, Dharma, Sangha and Mind.

I would not have known this from doing a retreat as we don't talk. I suppose it is interesting but unnecessary for practice.

> Eating meals together in silence is an important part of formal practice....The emphasis is on together action. We all eat the same food, regardless of each person's like or dislikes. Silence is kept not only by not talking, but also by making an effort to use the utensils gently and quietly.

During retreat, on a couple of occasions, Robert broke silence to remind us not to clang our bowls as we cleaned them. The rules include:

> Lay the bowls out on the square wrapping cloth in the following order, where D is the smallest bowl and A is the largest.
>
> D   C
> A   B
>
> Put your utensils in bowl C with their handles at 3 o'clock. Place the bowls in the center of the mat and always keep them touching during the meal.
>
> The first server will serve everyone water. When it is your turn to receive water, raise your bowl A with both hands, then rotate it back and forth when you've gotten enough. Pour the water into bowl C.

From this sample of rules for formal meals, you get a picture of how each step in the meal is prescribed. People attending retreats watch each other to learn the steps and process. However, we often are watching other people who may not have read the rules or forgotten them and so we may end up learning things not quite as they are described in the *Dharma Mirror*.

On Formal Meals

I invited my brother Nathan to join me on a Backroads biking research trip in the Dordogne region of France. He readily agreed to be my driver and companion in exchange for staying at elegant inns and chateaux, sampling gourmet meals and seeing the beautiful countryside while we traveled the back roads.

On our first night in the region, we ate dinner in the chateau's ornate dining room. Nathan ordered an entrée of roasted duck breast and I ordered *cassoulet*, a baked stew. After our first course, a waiter removed our plates and silverware and brought fresh silverware that was tucked inside a napkin sitting on a plate. He carefully placed each piece of new silverware in front us.

I noticed that Nathan and I now had different knives. Then two waiters brought our main courses, each plate covered with a silver lid. With a flourish, they lifted the covers of the entrées. The waiters looked down at the table then at each other with a look of horror on their faces. They then placed the covers back on our plates, stepped away from the table and left taking our entrées with them.

Nathan and I exchanged puzzled glances. Then a waiter quickly approached the table and removed our knives. He came back a few moments later with fresh knives. Then the other waiters came back and uncovered our plates with slightly less of a flourish and placed our entreés before us.

Nathan and I held our breaths so that we wouldn't laugh. Of course the waiters had no idea that we would not have had a clue that they had given us the wrong knives to accompany our entrée choices. The meal was delicious and the service impeccable, if not too attentive.

Just like at a formal meal at the Zen Center, there was a particular way that meals were served in the elegant dining rooms in France. For those in the know, it seemed to matter greatly that it was done with care and perfection. For those of us who didn't understand the protocol, it all seemed a bit over the top. As I ate more of these formal meals both in my travels and at the Zen Center, I began to understand the ways and follow along as best I could. Rather than judge the eating style, I chose to participate and learn what I could about and from these dining rituals. The formal meals became an opportunity to practice being present, observing my thoughts and actions as I ate and appreciating the food whether it was brown rice and vegetables or *cassoulet*.

Key to the Castle

Nathan and I were conducting our research in the Dordogne just a few days prior to the start of their spring tourist season. So at a couple of the chateaux that we were checking out for possible inclusion in future Backroads trips, we happened to arrive and stay with the owners a day prior to their opening to regular guests. They were busy uncovering furniture that had been draped with white cloth. They pulled antiques and silver out of closets to display on mantels and in cabinets. They inventoried their wine cellars.

At Chateau de la Treyne they were not serving dinner. We were disappointed as we wanted to experience their dining room.

The owners recommended that we eat at the café at the train station. Nathan and I thought this was an unusual and uninspired recommendation for dinner. As we got in our rental car, the lady of the house came out the front door of the chateau and ran up to the car holding something in her hand. Nathan rolled down the car window. She said, "We may be away when you return from dinner. Here is the key to our castle." The key was large and brass and just like you might imagine a key to a castle would look and feel. As she walked away, Nathan and I looked at each other once again in surprise.

"She just handed us the key to her castle."

We followed her directions to the train station and found it easily. This was not like the train station cafes we were used to in the United States. It was cozy with views of the surrounding hillsides at sunset. What I remember most about that dinner was that I ate the most delicious and fresh salad that I have ever eaten in my life. What a surprise treat. My preconceived notions of a train station dinner were rocked, and I was just trusted with the key to a castle. That was a memorable evening.

Chateau de la Treyne

Likes and Dislikes

Each day on the retreat we have a work period from 8:40–9:40 a.m. Just prior to the work period, the Zen Master will say something like, "we need two people to clean the Dharma room," and he will either assign two people or ask for volunteers. Then he'll go through the other jobs that need to be done and ask for volunteers or make assignments.

I have my preferred jobs. I like to garden when the weather is nice. Next I prefer cleaning the Dharma Room, and then cleaning the hall, entryway and lounge area. My least favorite job is cleaning the bathrooms. There was actually someone on the retreat who would volunteer to clean the bathrooms. I was surprised and grateful for this. It turns out his likes and dislikes are different from mine. After the retreat ended I thanked him for volunteering to clean the bathrooms. He said that was his preferred job. Who would have thought?

When I travel, I also have my likes and dislikes. I like to sit on the aisle of a plane so that it is easier to get up and stretch. I don't like touristy places that are all about shopping. I like to get off the beaten path. I don't like spending a lot of time driving in a car no matter how beautiful the scenery.

At the Zen retreat, I had plenty of time to pay attention to my likes and dislikes. I didn't like chanting. And then, chanting started to shift for me. For one, it did add variety to the day and evening. I also saw how it was another opportunity to practice. Practice what? Practice paying attention to my likes and dislikes. I learned to see chanting as a mirror. What is reflected back to me when I notice my reactions to chanting?

Some people in the room have beautiful voices for chanting, others chant off key. I have trouble getting my tongue around the words and find myself judging. When else do I judge myself and others? When do I let my likes and dislikes get in the way of being present? What do I want to do about that?

In the beginning,. I didn't understand what was going on during the formal meals and judged each part of the process. That judging mind again. Over time, I accepted the way it was and tried to just do it.

I served myself less food so that I finished eating close to when the Zen Master finished. I started to get the hang of the routine with the four bowls. I realized that meals were another mirror to reflect back my thinking and being. My likes and dislikes didn't matter. If I could participate fully in the eating, there were no likes and dislikes. I was just eating, in the Dharma room, with the other retreat members.

When I attended my very first retreat, I was shocked by the idea of the retreat leader hitting people on the shoulder blades with a stick. In the eight day retreat, I looked forward to when the head dharma teacher came by every other sitting period with the meditation stick. It was like getting a micro massage on my sore back. It also helped to wake me up if I felt sleepy. My first view of the stick fourteen years prior was as an implement of torture, now I saw it as a healing tool.

Recently I spent the night in the town of St. Augustine, Florida. A friend recommended the destination. I was surprised by how touristy the town was. At first I was disappointed. I didn't like it. Then I let that go and asked myself just to notice it and to find the beauty in it for me. We ended up walking through the side streets and along the waterfront away from the tourist shops. In the evening, we went to a piano bar to hear live music. Yes, we pursued the activities that we "liked" and we let go of our disappointment. We made the most of our time in St. Augustine. We managed not to let our likes and dislikes hijack our mini-vacation.

On Mindfulness
Do not cling to your opinions.
Do not go where you have no business.
Do not listen to talk which does not concern you.
Do not make the bad karma of desire, anger, or
    ignorance.
If in this lifetime you do not open your mind,
You cannot digest even one drop of water.

Don't Know

One of the primary teachings of Zen Master Seung Sahn is "don't know mind." Many of us who attended Empty Gate Zen Center in Berkeley were quite educated. We were either a student, a faculty or staff member, if not currently, at UC Berkeley or at one of the other institutions of higher learning in the area. We were trained to be thinkers, to read and analyze, to ask questions, to ponder, to debate, to be experts in our fields.

So what is this "don't know mind?" At the time, I was a manager. I was paid to know things, to share my knowledge with others, to be an expert. How was I to reconcile this seeming contradiction between my work and what I was learning at the Zen Center?

This was a concept that I struggled with for quite some time, and still do occasionally. I love learning. I love to read and see and do new things. Now, in my work I provide consulting and executive and life coaching services to adults. People pay me for my knowledge and experience. They also pay me to ask questions that get to the heart of an issue and that challenge them to look at themselves in new ways. In order for me to do that, I need to get quiet. I need to be present with the individual and pay attention. Now I practice "don't know mind" in my work on a regular basis.

The mantra that is offered to people who come to sit at the Empty Gate Zen Center is to repeat on the in-breath, "clear mind, clear mind, clear mind" and on the out-breath, "don't know."

"Clear mind" points to, "What is this? What do I see in front of me?" A brown floor. "What do I hear?" The sound of a car passing by. "What do I experience right now?" My seat on the cushion.

"Don't know" refers to before-thinking mind. By repeating "don't know" we are trained to let go of thinking, opinions and desires and to continually return to a questioning mind. "What is this? What am I?"

Zen Master Bon Soeng describes "Great Question," as one of the three foundations of Zen practice: Great Question, Great Courage, Great Faith. "Asking these great questions brings our meditation and mindfulness alive. As we sit in meditation, these questions bring energy and focus to our silent work."

By repeating "clear mind, clear mind, clear mind; don't know," it gives my mind a focus. When my mind wanders from these phrases and I catch myself making commentary on my experiences—judging, worrying, planning or any number of other thought patterns—I bring myself back to my breath and to the mantra.

This then frees me to be open to hearing new perspectives. I learn to not hold my own opinion so tightly (which causes stress when things don't go as I believe that they should). It also frees me to take action. Based on my clearer thinking, I have more energy to pursue that which matters for me and the community.

Looping Back

On a Backroads research trip for a potential new walking tour in Utah, I invited along Mark, who was still my boyfriend at that time, to be my research assistant. Our job was to check out hikes, national parks and accommodations in the Canyonlands and Arches areas of Utah. In my mind, it was also a way to "check out" Mark as a traveling companion. I already knew he could dance, now I could discover if we were compatible as travel and work partners.

One night we stayed at a new lodge near Canyonlands National Park. A friend of the owners, Jake, joined us for dinner that night in the small dining room. Throughout the evening he wove detailed stories about his travels into the conversation. He described how he never liked to "loop back," which for him meant traveling back the same way he came. He preferred to make a circle if he needed to go back to where he started. The details of his captivating stories have long since left my memory, but his idea of "looping back" has stuck with both Mark and me. When we are out on a trail hiking, we often look for ways to make a circular route rather than loop back; and if we do need to loop back, we will joke about it. "Oh no, we're looping back."

The funny thing is that when we do loop back, the trail looks different going the other way. We are seeing it from a new perspective. We will often comment that we didn't notice a particular tree or a path leading off the trail on the way out.

On the other hand, I think Jake was also being metaphorical. He tries to not keep going over the same territory in his thinking and behavior. Do I really want to keep thinking about this event or conversation over and over? How can I move on down the road in my mind?

Knowing when to loop back and when to move on can be tricky. How do I know when I have gone deeply enough in thinking about something? If I move on too quickly and gloss over an issue, I may find it comes back into my thoughts at a later time.

I have sat in meditation and replayed endlessly a conversation that I had with someone that did not go as I would have liked. This was particularly true when I was the Executive Director at Ashkenaz Music & Dance Community Center in Berkeley. The job was multifaceted. We had very few staff and I had many responsibilities. I reported to a diverse board of directors, the center had many constituencies, and we were faced with a limited budget. In addition, my mom's Alzheimer's disease was progressing and I was concerned about her. I was experiencing a lot of stress and felt a heavy weight on my shoulders that I didn't recognize at the time. Only later did I realize that my posture had also taken on this weight as my shoulders became hunched forward.

I was passionate about my work and doing what I thought was best for Ashkenaz. And, in hindsight I recognize that I didn't always listen to others very well. I sometimes would get in heated conversations that I later regretted. I would go to the Zen Center on Wednesday night and end up replaying a conversation over and over in mind as I sat in meditation. I would "loop back" over the conversation. Sometimes I felt bad about my behavior. Sometimes I was able to put myself in the shoes of the other person. Other times I achieved some clarity.

Often I would come up with a plan to speak to the person again under less heated conditions. By giving myself the opportunity to sit quietly, I was able to reflect and find some peace with the situation. Then, a way to move forward would become clear.

Strong Center

Zen Master Bon Soeng often says that we must develop a strong center. In Zen, we develop a strong center through meditation practice.

In Aikido, as in other martial arts, one also practices to develop a strong center. If you have a strong center, then you will not easily be knocked off balance by attacks or blows.

In dance, I was also taught to move from the center. We would practice walking across the floor on a diagonal as if led from our center. I studied the Martha Graham dance technique in college which emphasizes contraction and release, which originates from the center of the body. From this practice, I am free to move my limbs, isolate different parts of my body, twist and move with a range of motion that would not be available to me if I did not have a strong center.

Singers are taught to breathe from their diaphragm so that they are able to fill their entire upper body with air which allows them to have more control over their breath and their vocal quality.

THE KEY TO THE CASTLE

When making a ceramic pot on the wheel, you first need to center the clay. That is accomplished both with firmness and responsiveness to the clay. M.C. Richards writes:

> Centering: that act which precedes all others on the potter's wheel. The bringing of the clay into a spinning, unwobbling pivot, which will then be free to take innumerable shapes as potter and clay press against each other. The firm, tender, sensitive pressure which yields as much as it asserts.

In two documentary films about New Orleans Mardi Gras Indians, *Bury the Hatchet* and *Tootie's Last Suit*, I was struck by how the chiefs' practice of making their elaborate beaded and feathered suits was like a meditation. The chiefs designed, constructed and sewed a new suit each year. The process included many hours of sewing on each individual bead, rhinestone and feather that covered their body from toe to elaborate headdress. I wondered if this process of sitting and sewing helped these chiefs to develop a strong center.

When disaster struck after Hurricane Katrina and the breach of the levees, the three chiefs featured in the film, *Bury the Hatchet*, all soon came back to New Orleans and began work on rebuilding their homes and lives. They started making a new suit so that they could parade in Mardi Gras and be a symbol of strength for the community.

Was it a strong center that gave the Mardi Gras Chiefs the courage and drive to continue their traditions? Zen Master Bon Soeng reminds us to build a strong center so that when we most need it, as the Mardi Gras Chiefs did, we are able to call on it to help us get through the tough times.

Help Each Other

A guiding principle for sangha relationships at the Kwan Um School of Zen is to *help each other*. We do that in many ways—by practicing together, collectively maintaining the Zen center, by celebrating together and by making a commitment to help all beings in and outside of the sangha.

On the eight-day retreat during a work period early in the week, I was assigned to clean the dharma room with "Claire." Silently we gathered our supplies and decided who would do what by the tools that we each chose to use. She swept the cushions and the floor; I dusted the altar, windows and walls.

We had some time left prior to the bell ringing indicating it was time to end the work period. I started to dust the screen which hid the shelves holding extra cushions. Claire came over to help me. Between the two of us, we figured out an efficient technique to accomplish our task, all done silently.

This simple task of working together in silence contributed to a closeness between Claire and me. Through the act of helping each other, we felt a connection.

HELP EACH OTHER

In Zen Master Bon Soeng's dharma talks he often emphasizes that the larger purpose of our spending time in meditation is so that "we can find our true self and help this world." By finding our true self, we are able to help others in a way that is truly helpful. Not done out of obligation or out of a desire for self-promotion or to change someone else. I believe that my sitting practice has helped me to understand how I can help others in my everyday way of being in the world as well as in activities specifically designed to be of help. I consciously ask the questions: What would be helpful in this situation? Am I really helping?

One of my favorite books on this topic is *How Can I Help?* by Ram Dass & Paul Gorman. Written in 1985, I first discovered this book soon after that. I was working as a counselor and asking myself the questions, "What does it mean to be helpful? How do I, as a person in the 'helping professions,' take care of myself as I help others? How do I keep from getting overwhelmed by all of the suffering in the world?" This book was helpful to me then and still speaks to me today, such as this quote:

> The reward, the real grace, of conscious service, then, is the opportunity not only to help relieve suffering but to grow in wisdom, experience greater unity, and have a good time while we're doing it.

The Mind's Path

When I first started sitting, I had questions about the form and the practice of sitting. "Am I sitting correctly? Why do we sit with our left hand cupped in our right hand with the thumbs lightly touching? Why do we sit with our eyes open? Is it okay if I close my eyes? How do I bring my breath into my belly instead of my chest? What if I can't do that? How do I stop my thoughts? Is it okay to have thoughts? Why do we chant? What is the significance of the robes? What's with all of the rituals?" My questions went on and on. And the questions evolved over time.

In the beginning, I observed the form. Being a dancer, I have an eye for observing the body and copying body postures. However, I sometimes felt like rebelling. "I don't want to sit with my hands like that. In other meditation classes or groups, we sit with our hands on our knees or thighs. I like that better. So there!"

Mark and I would joke about my desire to rebel. I liked being different. I was an independent person and I would do what I wanted. I didn't really question this attitude. I just assumed that this is who I was and how I wanted to be. However I often felt a tension in this attitude. I wanted to be independent, yet I also wanted to follow the rules and fit in. I couldn't always get the right balance between those ways of being.

I can't pinpoint when this attitude shifted for me. At some point I stopped questioning things so much and went with the flow. The first wave of this "just being" with the practice was after I took the five precepts. The second wave came about half-way through the 8-day retreat. I stopped questioning everything and just sat. My mind became clearer and as Jeff suggested, I tried to make my mind more pointed. I had a few moments of this clarity during the retreat.

There was less striving in my practice. While I tried to bring my attention back to my breath, I was less concerned about "doing it right." I just let the practice be. I noticed that if I sat down with an intention to focus my thoughts in a certain way, often that was not where my thoughts would go. So, I allowed them to take their own shape and just watched. Then, I tried to bring myself back to my breath. It became easier to focus on my breath. I was learning to have more control over my thoughts.

I noticed that this transferred to other times in my day. I used to create tragic stories in my mind. If Mark was late getting home at night, I imagined a whole scenario of what might have happened to him, making up the entire scene in my mind. I couldn't seem to stop myself. I did the same with other family members.

But from my experience with meditation, I learned to watch my thoughts and bring myself back into the present moment. I discovered that I could do the same thing with my thoughts when I was not meditating. If I caught myself creating a story about something and playing an endless tape, I asked myself if I really wanted to go there. If not, I redirected my thoughts. This has been incredibly liberating. I no longer need to take myself down a path of "what if's" without intending to do so. I feel a sense of freedom in this new way of being with my mind.

Fantasy in the Dharma Room

Is it "okay" to write about this? Is there some secret bond among Zen practitioners that we don't talk or write about this sort of thing? Who knows? So, here I go.

As I sat in the retreat on Sunday, day three of the retreat, I suddenly had an understanding about the Tibetan tantric paintings and sculptures that I had seen in the San Francisco Asian Art Museum and on my travels in Nepal. These images of gods with their consorts are quite graphic and sexy. I often wondered about their place in temples and as "holy" objects of art. An experience sitting that afternoon gave me some new ways of thinking about these images.

It was perhaps the third round of sitting in the afternoon. I happened to look up at "Maurice" across the room. His eyes were closed and he had a smile on his face. He was swaying slightly in a circular fashion. I flashed that he was having a sexual fantasy. I realized that this may or may not be true, but then I thought, hey, I can go there too. No reason that he should have all of the fun. So, I took myself on a sexual fantasy. I was amazed at how quickly the pain in my body went away and instead I felt pleasure. Where did the pain go? Where did the pleasure come from?

It had never occurred to me before that people might have sexual fantasies on a meditation retreat! I am not sure why this is so, but then again I had never sat for this long before. Later I asked Mark if he had sexual fantasies on retreat and he said yes. I wondered if this is more common for men than women.

Back in the dharma room, I thought, now this could get addicting. Then I thought that sexual fantasies probably do not qualify as "clear mind." I was amazed that by directing my thoughts to a different area of my body I was able to relieve myself of pain, at least temporarily. I decided I would allow myself to go to this "special place" once per day on the retreat. Was this an example of "bargaining" with myself?

As I sat I wondered if the Tibetan artists/monks who made the explicit paintings came up with these images while meditating. Is there a long history of sexual fantasy during retreats?

When I brought myself back into the dharma room, into the present moment, I found myself telling a story about my retreat experience. "Do I share this experience when I give my dharma talk? Should I write about it? Where is the distinction between private and public? What would the purpose be of sharing this and alternatively what reason would I have for not sharing it?"

I did spend one sitting period, usually in the evening when my body hurt the most from sitting, enjoying a sexual fantasy. And, like the first time, I was able to divert my attention from my pain to pleasure, at least temporarily. I didn't go there every night, however. It wasn't a conscious decision to "deprive" myself. The idea to do so just didn't come to my awareness. The sexual fantasy became a tool for me to use to focus my attention. I am not sure that Zen Master Seung Sahn would have approved of this particular tool.

During the retreat, I also practiced *tonglen* meditation and *metta* as ways to help me focus my mind. I first learned about the Tibetan practice of tonglen meditation during my New Ventures West coach training program. One of the teachers gave me a practice of doing tonglen each day. At the time, I felt a lot of sadness about the health of several of my family members and friends, about my mom's Alzheimer's disease and about the state of the world. I listened to the news on the radio and tears welled up in my eyes. I felt the weight of the world's suffering.

The teacher thought that by practicing tonglen meditation, I could transform the sadness and awaken compassion for myself and others.

He directed me to Pema Chodron's books, *When Things Fall Apart*, and *Start Where You Are*, for an explanation of tonglen meditation.

> Tonglen practice is a method for connecting with suffering—our own and that which is all around us, everywhere we go. It is a method for overcoming our fear of suffering and for dissolving the tightness of our hearts. Primarily it is a method for awakening the compassion that is inherent in all of us, no matter how cruel or cold we might seem to be.

The practice of tonglen is done in four stages; more simply, it involves "breathe in and breathe out, taking in pain and sending out spaciousness and relief." I practiced tonglen meditation daily for a couple of months.

The tonglen practice was helpful to me at that point in my life. It helped me to focus my sadness and turn it around to compassion for myself and others. It is a meditation practice that I call upon occasionally as I did at some points during the eight-day retreat.

One of the first times I was exposed to metta (loving kindness meditation) was at a one day workshop at Spirit Rock Meditation Center in Marin County, CA. The workshop was led by Sylvia Boorstein and Stephen Cope. Sylvia offered us the following metta meditation and I have incorporated this in my own meditation practice at various times since then.

> May I be peaceful
> May I be happy
> May I be free of suffering

In my meditation, I repeat these phrases (or versions of them) to myself several times. Then, I extend the meditation beyond myself. During the eight day retreat, I repeated the phrases for everyone in the dharma room. Then I included my family and friends, then everyone in the Bay Area, in California, in the United States, in the World. By doing this metta meditation, it helped me focus my mind and feel a sense of loving kindness and connection with myself and others.

Metta, tonglen, focus on breath and the mantra, "clear mind, clear mind, clear mind – don't know," and even sexual fantasy were tools that helped me to direct my thoughts and to become "clearer and more pointed," as Jeff would say. Not all were Zen meditation tools, yet they were resources that helped me focus my mind during the long retreat.

Fantasy on a Backroads Vacation

Backroads offers special bicycling and hiking trip dates for singles and solos. I imagine that many of the singles fantasize that they will meet their future mate on vacation. Or, they may fantasize that on the trip they will meet someone to hang out with and enjoy during the vacation, whether it leads to anything in the future or not.

When I was a guest on the Baja trip I met a man with whom I hung out. I had brought with me Ann Rice's book, *Interview With A Vampire*, and for some reason we read it out loud to each other as we sat on the beach. We had a literary connection and that was the extent of our intimacy, which was fine with me.

That doesn't mean that was the extent of intimacy that I had on other Backroads trips. Like our guests, the trip leaders and staff at Backroads also fantasized about meeting someone special while on vacation or working in a beautiful location far from home.

Many Backroads leaders are now married to one another. It is not surprising. When you work together in an intense way, you learn how your coworker handles himself under pressure. You come to appreciate his ability to stay calm, to solve problems, to be creative, to communicate or not.

I was enlisted to co-lead the first New Mexico bicycling trip because I had done the work from the office to set up the trip. My co-leader happened to be a man with whom some of the female trip leaders found difficult to work. I thought, we have the entire drive from San Leandro, California to Santa Fe, New Mexico to get to know one another. I can work with this person.

As we were getting ready to pull the fully stocked van and trailer out of the loading area in San Leandro, "Charlie" asked if I would start the drive. I agreed. Once we got on the freeway, he climbed over the back of the front seat and said he was going to take a nap in the back seat, which he proceeded to do for the next six hours. My fantasy of getting to know him by the time we reached Santa Fe was not realized. And things went downhill from there.

The guests on this trip were amazing. They were adventurous, curious and a lot of fun. I cannot say the same about my experience with my co-leader. Thankfully, I was heading home after this trip and someone else, a male leader, was taking my place. My fantasy of working harmoniously with this leader didn't quite pan out as I had imagined. And that is the way life sometimes works out despite our best intentions.

What is a Sangha?

I didn't understand the idea of sangha until I felt it. In fact it was many years of going to the Empty Gate Zen Center before the meaning of sangha was clear to me. Now I understand it as a community of practitioners.

When I first started to go to the Zen Center and even prior to attending on a regular basis, I was leery about becoming part of an organized group. I told Mark that I was not a "joiner." I preferred to be independent. I liked my outsider status. As an undergraduate, I studied anthropology and was trained, in those days, to be an observer.

I now see that this was a lonely place for me. I yearned deep down, though I didn't admit it, to be a participant as well as an observer. I just was not aware of this desire at the time.

Now I believe it took deep sadness to bring me to the sangha. One of the first times that I attended a Saturday morning sitting at Empty Gate Zen Center was soon after Mark and I moved back to the Bay Area after caring for my mom in Santa Barbara. This was one of the most challenging times of my life as I watched my mom's mind change. It was also a time of watching my own mind and behaviors and those of my siblings as we dealt with this disease.

So when I went into the interview room on that Saturday morning with Zen Master Bon Soeng, and he had me read a Zen kong-an that is common to use with beginners, I immediately started to cry. I thought about my mom as I read that kong-an. Zen Master Bon Soeng asked me what had come up for me, and I shared with him that the kong-an made me think about my mom's situation, the inevitability of death and my sadness. He didn't make me try to "answer" the kong-an that time. He said that was enough. After that experience, I felt that the Zen Center was a place I could come to explore my feelings surrounding my mom's disease—both silently, and sometimes verbally.

The Human Route
Coming empty-handed, going empty-handed—that
   is human.
When you are born, where do you come from?
When you die, where do you go?
Life is like a floating cloud that appears.
Death is like a floating cloud that disappears.
The floating cloud itself originally does not exist.
Life and death, coming and going, are also like that.
But there is one thing that always remains clear.
It is pure and clear, not depending on life and death.
Then what is the one pure and clear thing?

These were the very questions that I was asking about my mom's life. These were the questions I was asking about my own life. And now I recognize that these were some of the questions that the Balinese villagers asked us as we pedaled our bikes past them on the road. "Where you from? Where you go?"

Mom in New Mexico

Attending the Zen Center helped me to deal with my grief, both before and after my mom's death. It helped me to understand my complicated feelings of guilt, shame for how I sometimes treated my mom as well as my love and sadness. I felt close to my siblings and husband as we each sought in our own ways to understand our relationship with our mom and with the disease. On Wednesday nights, during the question and answer period, I sometimes asked the Zen Master a question related to my mom and derived a bit of peace from his answer.

By attending Empty Gate more regularly, I started to feel a part of the community, the sangha. I started to recognize people and looked forward to seeing them even if we didn't talk much. At the conclusion of the Wednesday night programs, people would often stay and talk to one another. At first, I would often leave quickly after the program. But gradually, I started to stay and talk with people. After I took the five precepts, I welcomed newcomers, engaged them in conversation and let them know how the evening would unfold. I tried to help them feel welcome. I also took on occasional jobs at the Zen Center. Sometimes I did laundry, shopped for groceries prior to a retreat, developed flyers about our sitting schedule, and other miscellaneous tasks. I found that I did not lose my independence as I participated more. In fact, as I became a part of the Zen Center, I then had more personal courage. And after completing the eight-day retreat, though it was done in silence, I truly felt a part of the sangha.

Fly Away

One evening during dinner after we had lived with my mom for about a year, she and I told Mark about the visit we had had that day with her oldest friends, Joyce and Maury. Each Sunday I took mom to visit them at their home. On that particular day, when I picked mom up after her hour-long visit, I realized that Joyce was not having a good day. She was saying things that didn't make much sense. As we said goodbye to Joyce and Maury and their caregivers, mom and I both had tears in our eyes.

We got in the car and mom said, "Don't ever let me get like that." I said, "Mom, what am I supposed to do?" My nonviolent mom said, "Just shoot me." I told her, "I could get in trouble for that." She said, "I don't care."

At dinner that night, mom said, "Old people should just be allowed to fly away."

A few years later, I wrote this haiku:
>   Old people should just
>   be allowed to fly away,
>   my mother declared.

My mom died on a Wednesday morning five years later. I drove with my brother Robert from the Bay Area to the Central Coast of California to be with her for her passing. Mark stayed in the Bay Area and he asked that chanting be done for her that night at the Zen Center. My mom would have liked that, I am certain.

At mom's deathbed, Robert sang the chorus of "I'll Fly Away" and I joined in. I don't think Robert knew about mom's request to be allowed to fly away. And, I don't think mom was consciously aware of the song when she made her request five years earlier.

I'll Fly Away excerpt

Some glad morning when this life is o'er,
I'll fly away;
To a home on God's celestial shore,
I'll fly away (I'll fly away).

Chorus
I'll fly away, Oh Glory
I'll fly away; (in the morning)
When I die, Hallelujah, by and by,
I'll fly away (I'll fly away).

Synchronicity and Gurus

When I still frequented the local video rental store, prior to becoming a Netflix patron and the subsequent demise of the said video store (cause and effect?), I was browsing the shelves of videos. A documentary film caught my attention entitled, *Fierce Grace*. Directed by Mickey Lemle, it is about the life and teachings of Ram Dass, the aging process and his journey before and after his stroke. The film had a significant impact on me as I was grieving my mom's passing.

In one scene, Ram Dass sat with a young woman who had come to him for spiritual counsel. Her boyfriend had died and she was struggling with coming to terms with his death. Ram Dass was fully present with her and as she spoke and cried he shed his own tears along with her. I was struck by this. Counselors, psychologists, and coaches are taught to maintain a certain distance from their clients and to not express their own emotions during sessions.

This has often been difficult for me to do, though I try. Playing kickball in elementary school, tears would well up in my eyes when another child was hit hard by the ball. So seeing Ram Dass express emotion when listening and supporting this young woman, surprised and opened a door to another possibility for me.

Ram Dass had a stroke in 1997, and the film shows his process of dealing with this new development in his life. He eventually described this event as having "been stroked." He embraced the stroke and was able to feel a sense of comfort and grace in this next phase of his life.

Mark found for me at a used bookstore Ram Dass' classic book, *Be Here Now*, and I enjoyed reading this rather dated book again. I first read it in the 70's, introduced to it at that time by my older brother Robert. Then I read *Still Here: Embracing Aging, Changing, and Dying* which Ram Dass began writing prior to his stroke and was struggling to finish. Only after the stroke did the book come together in the way that he wanted.

Earlier in the year, Mark and I had gone to Oahu. Mark had a conference in Honolulu, so I tagged along since it was an opportunity to spend time bathed in the warmth and sweet smells of the islands. On the way to Hawaii, our flight was delayed by 5 hours out of Oakland, California. The airline actually gave us vouchers for another flight to be taken within the year. This was quite a surprise given how airlines normally treat you. This airline is now out of business, but not before we were able to go back to Hawaii. We are not in the habit of going to Hawaii, or any other vacation destination twice in one year, so this was quite exciting.

I suggested to Mark that we look for a yoga retreat in Hawaii. He agreed with some trepidation. Not long after that, I was looking through *Yoga Times Magazine* and saw an ad for a workshop in Maui with Ram Dass (who lives on Maui), Sharon Salzberg, Krishna Das and Mark Whitwell. This looked intriguing as it was not long after my reading Ram Dass' books and seeing the documentary about him.

We were familiar with Krishna Das as we had attended a couple of *kirtan's* he led in San Francisco. *Kirtan* is the practice of chanting the names of the Hindu gods. Krishna Das sings a line, and then the audience sings it after him in a call and response fashion. It is a form of meditative practice. We have a couple of his CD's and are mesmerized by his voice. Mark, being a singer, was especially intrigued to go to a small workshop that included Krishna Das and the opportunity to sing each day.

I had heard of Sharon Salzberg but had not yet read any of her books nor had I heard her speak. The foundations of her work are mindfulness (*vipassanana*) and loving kindness (*metta*). She co-founded the Insight Meditation Society in Massachusetts. I was eager to meet and learn from her.

Mark Whitwell is a yoga teacher with deep roots in yoga, and he was to teach two yoga classes each day.

Then we learned that the Dalai Lama was going to be on Maui the two days following the retreat and would be speaking at the outdoor stadium in Wailuku. That was the deciding factor for us.

Mark and I had never done anything quite like this three-day workshop with four "gurus." We decided to jump in and try it. Mark joked that we might not need an airplane to fly home. We both wondered if the retreat would be "cult like?" Would we fit in?

I think that we also knew this could be a healing time for us as both of our mothers had died the previous year. We knew that Ram Dass would talk about aging and death and these were important topics for us at this time in April 2007.

During the workshop, we stayed at the Hale Akua Shangri-La Retreat Center which was also where the workshop was held. In a former incarnation it had been a center for tantric meditation. Throughout the grounds were statues of Hindu goddesses, fountains, a stream with a lily pond, and sculptures of couples in erotic embraces. As we registered the first day, we were given a wrist band to wear throughout the three days. Mark asked "What are these for?" The young woman at the table looked him in the eye and replied, "They are to indicate you are a member of the cult." While we knew she was teasing us, Mark and I looked at each other and gulped.

Sharon Salzberg's talks centered on the topic of loving kindness. "Loving kindness is seeing things clearly and being connected with oneself and others. The antithesis of loving kindness is the separation from self and others." Salzberg told us. "Meditation is the process of letting go and starting over each moment in tranquility and alertness. From practicing meditation, clarity and spaciousness emerges."

I observed myself during the early part of the workshop and noticed how I felt separate from others. I had a yearning for connection and yet that was not what I was experiencing.

Ram Dass shared that he was focusing on two topics at that point in his life: death and aging. He said, "I want to be a joyful aging role model. Old age is a chance to go inside because I can't go outside much." He suggested that we are able to go through life lightly if we don't identify with roles. Being with Ram Dass, as he sat in his wheel chair, was a gift. He shared his thoughts, joy and tears. He talked about his guru, Maharaj-ji, and in a lengthy ceremony he gave each of us, one by one, a *mala* (beads to use in meditation) while invoking the spirit of his guru. All the while

Krishna Das chanted during this 3-hour, surprisingly moving ceremony. Then later that day, we went swimming in the pool with Ram Dass.

Mark and I left the retreat filled with the wisdom of these wonderful teachers. By the end of the retreat, I also felt more of a connection with myself and the other participants. I believe that happened by letting go of preconceived ideas and roles just as Ram Dass and Sharon Salzberg discussed.

We headed upcountry for three more nights on our own at Olinda Country Cottages & Inn, with amazing views of the island and the ocean off in the distance. The grounds included a protea flower farm where I photographed these exotic flowers. We felt full from the three intense days of talks, meditation, yoga, chanting, and being with others we had never met before. We started to wonder if we really wanted to see the Dalai Lama the next day and be in the crowds and heat of the stadium. Maybe it was time to head to the beach. Is there such a thing as too much spirituality?

The next morning at the B&B we shared our thoughts with the other guests who had flown to Maui from the Big Island just to see the Dalai Lama. They looked at us like we were crazy. "How could you not want to see the Dalai Lama?" They convinced us that it would be worth it. And they were right. While the stadium was full, we did not experience crushing crowds. Yes, it was hot and there was little shade. And, I experienced such peace being in the presence of the Dalai Lama. His talk was on the teaching, "Eight Verses for Training the Mind," by the 11th-century meditator Geshe Langri Thangpa. The written program described, "These teachings represent the core of developing wisdom, compassion, and loving-kindness and offer techniques for destroying self-cherishing." These were themes that continued our learning from earlier in the week.

His talk was not easy to follow, yet the crowd on this weekday afternoon, sat quietly and attentive. I marveled at how we all just seemed to want to be in the presence of the Dalai Lama. I was overwhelmed with a feeling of hope, being in that amphitheater with 7000 people all there to hear this little man talk about peace, loving kindness and Buddhist teachings.

At one point I went to a tent that had been set up in order to get out of the sun. Once I squeezed in, I realized that it was for parents and their babies and young children. Even here it was quiet.

This week proved to be such a healing time for us. Being in the beauty of the island, soaking in the messages of these wonderful teachers, relaxing on the beach, meditating, chanting and doing yoga—it was just what we needed. We returned home with a sense of peace and understanding about our relationships with our moms.

Fast forward a couple of years. My coaching client, Lisa, tells me she is going on vacation in Maui. I ask her if she has heard of Ram Dass. She had some knowledge and interest in him. I shared with her that he now lives on Maui and occasionally gives public talks or invites people to join him at workshops.

A few weeks later, upon her return from Maui, she tells me a story. She and her partner were at the beach and she is reading Ram Dass' book, *Still Here*. At some point, she looks up from the book and sees an older man in the ocean with two other people next to him. She goes back to reading. Later she looks up and sees that the two people are helping the older man out of the water. He has a baseball cap on. Then she notices a wheel chair on the beach. She thinks to herself how it is great that he is able to enjoy the water. At some point he takes off his hat for a few moments and she sees his bald head with gray curly hair around the edges. She thinks, "Could that be Ram Dass?" She looks at the cover of her book with his photo. She asks her partner, "Do you think that is Ram Dass?" They agree that it could be.

Lisa gets up, with her book in hand, and walks to the edge of the water. Lisa says, "Hello, are you Ram Dass?" "Yes," he says. Lisa tells him, "I am reading your book at this very moment. I am so happy to meet you." Ram Dass seems quite moved by this. Now Lisa's partner comes to them and asks if she can take a photo of them. Ram Dass' assistant says, "This is really quite remarkable because we hardly ever come to this beach as it is on the opposite side of the island from where we live." There is an unsaid belief that this meeting was meant to be.

As Lisa shared this story with me, we both had tears in our eyes. We were grateful that she had this moving experience and marveled at the synchronicity.

New Destination

When I travel to a new place, whether to Ashland, Oregon or Ubud, Bali, at some point during the trip I imagine what my life might be like in this new place. How would I spend my days, with whom would I interact, would I find people of like mind, what could I learn here about myself and others? What is the weather like, the food, the physical environment?

These questions give me the opportunity to imagine myself other than as a tourist. What is life like for the people who live there throughout the seasons? How does life differ depending upon the economic or social class of the person? What is the role of women in this culture? What opportunities would I have for work?

Sometimes I ask myself these questions as I take a walk and come up with possible answers without doing any research. Sometimes I talk to people who live there to get more of a sense of their daily lives. Sometimes I read about the place. Asking questions helps me to think more deeply about what it might be like to live in this place and gives me a greater appreciation for the people. I also think more about what is important to me in how I live.

Mark and I traveled to Louisiana in October of 2009 for the Louisiana Book Festival where Mark presented his book, *Cajun and Zydeco Dance Music in Northern California: Modern Pleasures in a Postmodern World*. At first I wasn't going to go with Mark, but at the last minute decided to join him.

We had a wonderful trip – walking, exploring, and eating our way through New Orleans, boating in the Atchafalaya Basin on a swamp tour in Cajun Country, and listening to many writers read their works at the book festival in Baton Rouge, the state capitol. I particularly enjoyed hearing Ernest J. Gaines speak after having recently reread his book, *The Autobiography of Miss Jane Pittman*. As I sat in the Senate Chamber in the swivel seat of a state senator, the woman next to me asked where I was from. We had a lively conversation and she introduced me to other people sitting close to us.

This was not the first time on this trip that the people I met were super friendly. As we drove around, I asked myself "what would it be like to live here?"

I write a monthly e-newsletter. My most popular newsletter to date, judging by the number of people who sent me email messages after reading it, was the story I wrote entitled, "Working in the field you love when you can't get a job in your field."

The piece described how my husband pursued his academic and musical interests as an independent scholar because he had not secured a tenure track position at a university. He would get up early in the morning, prior to going to his administrative job, to read, write and practice his music. He developed a rich and satisfying life.

Fast forward two years and guess what? The dream job appeared out of nowhere, an endowed chair position to create a program in traditional music at the University of Louisiana at Lafayette.

When Mark forwarded the job announcement to me my first reaction was, "Wow, what a perfect fit." Then I thought about what it would be like to live in Lafayette, Louisiana. Since we had visited Louisiana in October, I had recent positive associations with the area. However, I had never lived in the South nor had any desire to, quite frankly.

I work as a life and career coach and in that role I support my clients in identifying and pursuing their dreams. How could I not support Mark in his dream? At the same time, I was aware that I needed to take care of myself and ensure that I could pursue my career and my happiness. I began to watch my thoughts and emotions as things progressed. When Mark was invited to have a Skype interview, I knew that the possibility of moving to Louisiana was now more of a reality. I was happy for him.

Then I had two days of mourning. I felt much like I did after my mom died. I cried. I was incredibly tired and sad. I watched what was happening and let myself be. I thought about the things that I would miss in my life in the San Francisco Bay Area: my friends and neighbors, my beautiful home and garden, Empty Gate Zen Center, all of the contacts and relationships that I had built in my work life. I had a good life and I was happy.

Then two days later I was back to normal. I realized that happiness is an inner state of being. If he was offered the job, we would build a new life in Louisiana while maintaining our friendships in California and around the country. Would we miss California at times? Yes, and we would go back to visit.

In February of 2010 I was planning to sit the Empty Gate Zen Center's eight-day retreat for the second time. That decision was made before Mark learned about and applied for the position in

Louisiana. Subsequently, he was invited for a campus interview and I was also invited to Louisiana. I think the interviewing committee wanted to make sure that I was on board with this possible move in case Mark was offered the job. So, instead of sitting the entire retreat, we just sat on Friday and Saturday as we had much to do to prepare for the interview and our journey.

In those two days of sitting, I did a lot of thinking. I thought about the mechanics of moving and ran through scenarios of how we might transport our cat. I thought about how I would miss the *sangha* and the opportunity to sit with this group and listen to Jeff's dharma talks. I felt excited about the possibilities for our lives and fearful as well.

This was a very different "sitting" experience than when I did the eight-day retreat. Perhaps if I had had the opportunity to sit for more than two days, my mind would have settled down. I was back to planning and calculating as I had in the first two days the year prior.

Mark was offered the position and accepted it with my support. Now my fantasy about what it would be like to live in Louisiana had taken on the realm of reality.

Just as friends were surprised that I planned to sit an eight-day retreat, people were surprised that we were moving to Louisiana. I think that some of my friends felt sorry for me. Moving from the San Francisco Bay Area to South of the South seemed like such a big leap. Even the Zen Master seemed skeptical about what our lives would be like.

After we moved, friends and sangha members asked how we were doing. I think some people expected us to be unhappy.

It seems I was ready for this next adventure. In no small measure, I believe that my Zen practice prepared me for this latest journey and has been a help and resource as I navigate life in the South. I take one day, one moment at a time. I ask myself, "what is this?" "what am I?" and when I answer, "Don't know," it feels true.

Open Door/Empty Gate

Some beginnings are by seeming accident and others seem to fit a plan. My first introduction to taiko drumming was by accident. I was walking in Central Park in New York City on a sweltering Sunday summer afternoon in 1982. A group of people were standing and using sticks to hit drums of various sizes positioned on stands. As they hit the drums, their body and arm movements were as much a dance as they were about making sound. I was mesmerized by those rhythms, sounds and movements.

When I returned to the Bay Area, I spotted in the newspaper that a taiko drumming group was performing at the Cherry Blossom Festival in Japantown in San Francisco. I headed to the city and again was entranced by the taiko. After the performance I stuck around and asked a member of the group whether they offered classes. She told me to show up at one of their rehearsals. I didn't need to call first, just come.

The rehearsals took place on a weekday evening in a small, dark room in the basement of a community center across the street from Japantown. At the time, it was a dicey neighborhood. My presence was not acknowledged when I entered the room. The teacher was Seiichi Tanaka, who started San Francisco Taiko Dojo in 1968 and has since built it to be a major school of taiko in the United States. At the time I visited, taiko was still being discovered in San Francisco. There were perhaps eight people at that rehearsal.

Tanaka shouted at the group, "Go outside and run around the block. You need to be in good shape in order to play taiko." I didn't know what to do. I stood for a few minutes to see if he would say hello to me. He did not. So, not being dressed for a jog, I went outside for a few minutes before re-entering the room when the others came back.

It was extremely loud as they played the drums together and the sound bounced off of the cement walls. Tanaka did not "break down" the pieces. They just played. I wondered how in the world I would learn to play in this kind of learning environment. I stayed for an hour and then quietly slipped out of the room and never went back.

The teacher opened the door, but I chose not to go through it. He didn't open the door very wide; however. I believe he was measuring my dedication, my drive to learn. Taiko is not an easy practice. It takes strength, both physical and mental. Now I look back and imagine that I was not ready for the challenge at that point in my life. I didn't have the drive.

We make our own choices about which doors we enter. Do I only enter doors where I am welcomed with open arms or do I sometimes enter places that require more effort on my part? The Chinese proverb says, "Teachers open the door. You must enter by yourself."

Not only must I enter, but I must decide whether to stay. Then I must continue to show up and participate and keep showing up even when it gets hard.

Empty Gate Zen Center front door

This is one of the primary lessons that I have learned from practicing Zen. To ask myself, how am I showing up? What are my thoughts, actions, feelings in this moment? How do I choose to be, to live in this moment? Am I willing to keep showing up when life gets tough?

"The great way has no gate." Richard Shrobe wrote in his book, *Don't Know Mind: The Spirit of Korean Zen*. "Great way doesn't mean greater than anything else. Great here has the connotation of complete. To realize the complete way is to be completely in touch with what is, moment by moment; not to be holding back and living in some imaginary world of shackles, chains, fantasies, yearnings, hopes, longings, regrets, and all the other things we get caught up in. The great way has no gate."

The Zen Center in Berkeley, CA, where I opened the door, walked in and sat down on the cushion, is called Empty Gate Zen Center. How can a gate be empty? There are physical gates that are made of wood or metal. They may have a lock on them that inhibit our ability to go through them or that require a key or a special combination. We also have mental gates upon which we place our own locks. Through our thoughts, we decide that we cannot enter certain places. These may be real or imagined. At Empty Gate Zen Center, we are given the opportunity to investigate, through meditation, our personal gates and learn whether and when to open, close and empty them.

Diana Lynch, one of the founders of Empty Gate Zen Center, answered my email about how the Zen Center got its name in a surprising way. "Soen Sa Nim was giving a dharma talk one night when we were first starting on Hillcrest Road, and his English was not so hot in those days! I am sure he meant to say "gateless gate" but "empty gate" came out instead and stuck. And I decided to call our newly forming Zen center that!"

In travel, I experienced many "gates" or obstacles. In France, my boyfriend and I tried to get from Paris to Avignon with our bikes on the same train that we were traveling. The train agent said "no" to each of our questions. Many gates were being placed in front of us. At one point, exasperated with us, he said, "No, no, no, no, NO!" with emphasis on the 5th "no." That is a phrase that has stuck with me for many years. When Mark and I are frustrated with someone's answer or when we want to emphasize a point, we jokingly use that rhythm of five "no's". In the end, we did find a way to travel with our bikes to our destination; however, on a more circuitous route than we had originally planned.

When Mark and I arrived in Santa Barbara and ended up taking care of my mom for two years as she faced Alzheimer's disease, it was an unplanned journey for all of us. It was a time of sadness and also an opportunity to practice compassion. A gate opened and we did not close it. I had no way of knowing at the time that stepping through that gate with trust would allow me to learn so much about myself and others.

Many of the gates that I have faced on my travels have now ended up in this book. They are the travel experiences that most stand out in my mind. From the bikes arriving very late in France for the first Backroads European tour, to the faulty brakes on our bus in Nepal, to the flat tire on a lonely road in Patagonia, to the King of Nepal taking our plane so that we ended up spending four nights in Bangkok instead of one on our way to Kathmandu, to attempting to find my way in traffic in downtown Santiago, Chile. During each of these vehicular experiences, I was given the opportunity to stop and be present. To take a breath and ask myself how do I want to be in this moment? What are my choices? What can I learn from this experience? How can I trust myself and this process?

In Nepal, our Sherpa guide cut us a walking stick to use to help us as we climbed a steep slope at high altitude. He instructed us to take one step at a time and to breathe. Once we got to our destination, we turned around and looked back over the mountains and valleys from where we had come. We had traveled far.

The Great Way Has No Gate

The Great Way has no gate,
A thousand roads enter it.
When one passes through this gateless gate,
He freely walks between heaven and earth.

By Wu Men (Hui-k'ai) (1183–1260)
Translated from Chinese by Eiichi Shimomisei

Circle Talk

At the end of the retreat, during circle talk, our Zen Center has a tradition of clapping for the people who have completed their first 8-day retreat. I wasn't aware of this tradition. So when everyone clapped for me when it was my time to speak, I was both surprised and proud. I felt like I had traveled significant distances on that retreat.

Now when I go to the Empty Gate Zen Center, I feel a part of a community of people with a common interest and focus. I now live in Louisiana and have only been back to Empty Gate a few times since I moved. However, I still feel a part of that community. And I imagine that if I were to go to another Kwan Um School of Zen center, I would feel a part of that sangha as well.

What makes it feel like community are certainly the people. It is also the practice and the forms that we all share in common. I am guessing that it is similar for a Catholic who feels comfortable and a part of a community no matter which Catholic Church she visits. I live in a Catholic part of the United States now. There is no Kwan Um School of Zen here. However, my experience of being connected to the Zen center community helps me to feel connected to all of my neighbors. While my own practice now is more solitary, I know that I am a part of many communities.

After having completed and survived an eight-day retreat, I now marvel at people who do 30 or 90 day retreats. How do they do that? Why do they do that? Who knows, maybe one day I too will go on a 30 day vacation; I mean retreat.

Chapter Notes

A Note on Names: When an individual's name appears in quotes, it means the name of the person was changed. Their name is written in quotes only the first time used.

Empty Gate Zen Center

Kwan Um School of Zen website, http://www.kwanumzen.org/about-us/, accessed 1/9/2012.

Spontaneity in Bali

Empty Gate Zen Center website, Zen Master Bon Soeng. *August 9, 2009.* "True Self, Authentic Self." http://emptygatezen.com/empty-gate-zen-center/?page=2, accessed 1/9/2012.

Morning Bows

Dharma Mirror, Greeting Bow, page 2.7.

Five Precepts

Dharma Mirror, Five Precepts, page 5.8.

Dharma Mirror, Temple Rules, page 6.3.

Calculating

Dharma Mirror, Temple Rules, page 6.5.

Walking Meditation

Dharma Mirror, version 2-92, Meditation, page 6.21.

Zen Buddhism: In Search of Self, Produced and Directed by Gong Jae-Sung.

Awakening Joy

When I attended the Awakening Joy course in 2009, it was a 10-month class. It is now a 5-month course. http://www.awakeningjoy.info/

Thousand Hands and Eyes Sutra, Perceive World Sound: Daily Chanting and Ceremonies of the Kwan Um School of Zen, Empty Gate Zen Center chant book, (Version developed by Dharma Zen Center, Los Angeles, CA), page 15 and page 1.

The Third Day

Original Face by Zen Master Seung Sahn, *The Whole World Is A Single Flower: 365 Kong-ans for Everyday Life, with questions and commentary by Zen Master Seung Sahn*. Charles E. Tuttle Company, Inc., Boston, 1992, page 111.

Chitwan Jungle in Nepal

Dharma Mirror, Temple Rules, page 6.6.

Laughter in the Dharma Room

Dharma Mirror, page 2.24 and 2.25.

Likes and Dislikes

Dharma Mirror, Temple Rules, page 6.3.

Don't Know

CHAPTER NOTES

Empty Gate Zen Center website, Zen Master Bon Soeng. *August 9, 2009.* "True Self, Authentic Self." http://emptygatezen.com/empty-gate-zen-center/?page=2, accessed 1/9/2012.

Centering

M.C. Richards, *Centering,* Wesleyan University Press, Connecticut, page 9.

Bury the Hatchet, Produced and Directed by Aaron Walker

Tootie's Last Suit, Produced and Directed by Lisa Katzman

Help Each Other

Ram Dass & Paul Gorman, *How Can I Help? Stories and Reflections on Service,* Alfred A. Knopf, New York, 1985, page 16.

Fantasy in the Dharma Room

Pema Chodron, *When Things Fall Apart: Heart Advice for Difficult Times,* Shambhala, Boston, 2000, page 93.

Pema Chodron, *Start Where You Are: A Guide to Compassionate Living,* Shambhala, Boston, 2001, pages 38-39.

What is a Sangha?

"The Human Route," by Zen Master Seung Sahn, copyright © Kwan Um School of Zen, is reprinted by permission of the Kwan Um School of Zen.

Fly Away

I'll Fly Away, Albert E. Brumley, © Copyright 1932 in "Wonderful Message" by Hartford Music Co. Renewed 1960 by Albert E. Brumley & Sons/SESAC (admin by ClearBox Rights). All rights reserved. Used by permission.

Synchronicity and Gurus

Fierce Grace, Produced and Directed by Mickey Lemle

Open Door/Empty Gate

Richard Shrobe, *Don't Know Mind: The Spirit of Korean Zen,* Shambhala, Boston & London, 2004, page 49.

Poetry Chaikhana website, The Great Way has no gate, http://www.poetrychaikhana.com/W/WuMenHuikai/GreatWayhasn.htm, accessed 2/1/2013.

Resources

As a beginning student of Zen, this book represents my personal experiences only. I encourage readers who would like to learn more about Zen and Buddhism to seek out a teacher and a Zen Center at which to practice. The following books and websites were referred to in the text or used in my research and may be of interest to readers.

Books

Awakening Joy: 10 Steps to Happiness by James Baraz and Shoshana Alexander (Parallax Press, Berkeley, California, 2012)

Cajun and Zydeco Dance Music in Northern California: Modern Pleasures in a Postmodern World by Mark F. DeWitt (University of Mississippi Press, Jackson, MS, 2008)

Centering by M. C. Richards (Wesleyan University Press, Middletown, CT, 1962)

Compass of Zen by Zen Master Seung Sahn (Shambhala, Boston & London, 1997)

Dharma Mirror: Manual of Practice Forms, Second edition edited by Merrie Fraser (The Kwan Um School of Zen, 1994, updated 2011)

Don't-Know Mind: The Spirit of Korean Zen by Richard Shrobe (Shambhala, Boston & London, 2004)

Dropping Ashes on the Buddha: The Teaching of Zen Master Seung Sahn compiled and edited by Stephen Mitchell (Grove Press, Inc., New York, 1976)

How Can I Help? Stories and Reflections on Service by Ram Dass & Paul Gorman (Alfred A. Knopf, New York, 1985)

Peace Is Every Step: The Path of Mindfulness in Everyday Life by Thich Nhat Hanh (Bantam Books, New York, 1991)

Still Here: Embracing Aging, Changing, and Dying by Ram Dass (Riverhead Books, New York, 2000)

The Whole World Is A Single Flower: 365 Kong-ans for Everyday Life with questions and commentary by Zen Master Seung Sahn (Charles E. Tuttle Company, Inc., Boston, 1992)

When Things Fall Apart: Heart Advice for Difficult Times by Pema Chodron (Shambhala, Boston, 1997)

Wherever You Go There You Are: Mindfulness Meditation in Everyday Life by Jon Kabat-Zinn (Hyperion, New York, 1994)

Zen Mind, Beginner's Mind: Informal talks on Zen meditation and practice by Shunryu Suzuki (Weatherhill, New York & Tokyo, 1970)

RESOURCES

Websites

Awakening Joy - http://www.awakeningjoy.info/

Backroads - http://www.backroads.com/

Empty Gate Zen Center - http://emptygatezen.com/

Kwan Um School of Zen - http://www.kwanumzen.org/

New Ventures West - http://www.newventureswest.com/

San Francisco Zen Center - http://www.sfzc.org/

Sharon Salzberg - http://www.sharonsalzberg.com/

Spirit Rock Meditation Center - http://www.spiritrock.org/

Gratitude

Heartfelt thanks to…

Mom who showed me the value of lifelong learning and that it was okay to be different.

Dad who demonstrated the value of work, keeping a budget and, through his example, that it was okay to have many careers.

Siblings Robert, Betty and Nathan for their love and partnership in this ongoing family journey.

Friends and fellow book group members who have enriched my life and are too numerous to mention by name.

Members and fellow practitioners at the Empty Gate Zen Center, I thank you deeply for sitting with me in the dharma room and especially to Zen Master Bon Soeng from whom I have learned so much. I hope that I have been true to your teachings, words and intent.

The community of dancers, musicians, and staff at Ashkenaz Music & Dance Community Center.

Friends and colleagues at Backroads and especially to Tom Hale.

New Ventures West founders, James Flaherty and Stacy Flaherty.

Writing Down Dementia workshop participants and to co-leader, Kim.

Carolyn, Christian, Darrell, Jeff, Jill, Linda, Lisa P, Lisa R, Mark, Mary, Peggy, Peter, Renee, Robert, Sandra, Suzy, and Tom for graciously reading drafts of the book and/or chapters and giving me your thoughtful comments.

My coaching and consulting clients: you help me stay engaged and curious each day.

Thank you, all.

Sue Schleifer, born in Santa Barbara, California, currently resides in Lafayette, Louisiana. Through her company, Oak Communications, she provides life and executive coaching and management consulting services to individuals and organizations around the country. She writes a monthly e-newsletter and has written for newspapers. She co-designed and facilitates ongoing *Writing Down Dementia* workshops. *Key to the Castle* is her first book.

Find her online at:
www.facebook.com/KeyToTheCastleBook

To learn about Oak Communications Coaching and Consulting:
www.Oak-Communications.com

www.ingramcontent.com/pod-product-compliance
Lightning Source LLC
LaVergne TN
LVHW051115080426
835510LV00018B/2049